The Art of SERIES
EDITED BY CHARLES BAXTER

The Art of series is a line of books reinvigorating the practice of craft and criticism. Each book is a brief, witty, and useful exploration of fiction, nonfiction, or poetry by a writer impassioned by a singular craft issue. *The Art of* volumes provide a series of sustained examinations of key, but sometimes neglected, aspects of creative writing by some of contemporary literature's finest practitioners.

THE ART OF

DESCRIPTION

WORLD INTO WORD

Other Books by Mark Doty

The Art of

DESCRIPTION

WORLD INTO WORD

Mark Doty

Graywolf Press

"An Enormous Fish" first appeared, in Spanish, in *Critica*.

"Speaking in Figures" first appeared in *American Poet*, the biannual journal of the Academy of American Poets, and was adapted from a lecture Mark Doty gave for the Online Poetry Classroom Summer Institute. Copyright © 2007 by The Academy of American Poets. All rights reserved.

This publication is made possible by funding provided in part by a grant from the Minnesota State Arts Board, through an appropriation by the Minnesota State Legislature, a grant from the National Endowment for the Arts, and private funders. Significant support has also been provided by Target; the McKnight Foundation; and other generous contributions from foundations, corporations, and individuals. To these organizations and individuals we offer our heartfelt thanks.

NATIONAL ENDOWMENT FOR THE ARTS

MINNESOTA STATE ARTS BOARD

WELLS FARGO

TARGET.

Published by Graywolf Press
250 Third Avenue North, Suite 600
Minneapolis, Minnesota 55401
All rights reserved.

www.graywolfpress.org

Published in the United States of America

ISBN 978-1-55597-563-0

4 6 8 9 7 5

Library of Congress Control Number: 2010920769

Cover design: Scott Sorenson

Contents

For the Eye altering alters all.

—William Blake

We delight in our sensuous involvement with the materials of language, we long to join words to the world—to close the gap between ourselves and things—and we suffer from doubt and anxiety because of our inability to do so.

—Lyn Hejinian

THE ART OF

DESCRIPTION

WORLD INTO WORD

It sounds like a simple thing, to say what you see. But try to find words for the shades of a mottled sassafras leaf, or the reflectivity of a bay on an August morning, or the very beginnings of desire stirring in the gaze of someone looking right into your eyes, and it immediately becomes clear that all we see is slippery, nuanced, elusive. As Susan Mitchell says, "The world is wily, and doesn't want to be caught."

Perception is simultaneous and layered, and to single out any aspect of it for naming is to turn your attention away from myriad other things, those braiding elements of the *sensorium*—that continuous, complex response to things perpetually delivered by the senses, the encompassing sphere that is such a large part of our subjectivity. The word always makes me think of a label invented to describe the totalizing experience offered by a kind of movie speakers, *Sensurround*—a commercial coinage, but a memorable one, in that it addresses the way we're englobed entirely by the reports of our senses, held in a kind of continuous thrall. A seamless weft of information—but *information* is the driest and least revealing of essential twenty-first-century words, and the data the senses offer every waking moment is anything but that.

In his memoir *Planet of the Blind,* Stephen Kuusisto describes a moment in Grand Central Station when he and his guide dog have just gotten themselves lost in the great urban hive of transport. Steve sees a dark, suggestive blur of shapes and colors; I want to write the word *only* or *merely* before *dark, suggestive blur,* but that isn't right. The way he sees is in fact a rich, engaging way of encountering the world, and that's Steve's point. His dog is new to the intricate passageways of the station, crowded with ranks of commuters streaming forward at a breathless pace, and Steve could reasonably be terrified. Instead he reports this as an occasion of pleasure, a perceptual adventure; both he and his companion animal are exhilarated, and having, as we say, the time of their lives.

In fact all perception is limited, no matter how acute your eyesight, how sharp the hearing, how sensitive the sense of touch. What we can take in is a partial rendering of the world. To go for a walk with a dog is enough to illustrate this principle. Where a universe of scents— historical, multifaceted—presents itself to the canine "reader," human nostrils detect maybe a little whiff of urine, maybe nothing at all. And dogs, in their turn, seem to be unable to see as we do. Their eyesight is geared to detect motion, the slightest bit of action, but when things are at rest they lack the ability to distinguish colors and patterns that human eyes might. Deer cannot see red or orange, a biologist writes, but apparently can see blue much better than we can. Who can even imagine what that would mean, for blue to be— well, more?

All accounts, it seems, are partial; thus all perception might be said to be tentative, an opportunity for interpretation, a guessing game.

On a warm August evening on a pier in Cherry Grove, New York, I watched a display of fireworks. The wooden dock was crowded, everyone excited for the show to start. Police boats and fire boats whizzed around on the water. When the first flare went up, it became clear that the barge from which the rockets flared was anchored a mere hundred yards off the end of the pier. We could see, in a way I never really did before, the rough industrial-looking process of firework-shooting. When a group of streaks all went up at once, the metal barge itself was lit, and you could smell the gunpowder, and see the fire fountains sputtering into action.

Proximity to the source meant that the shells were exploding right over our heads. A few children had to be comforted, a few shocked pets hurried away, but everyone else loved it, craning their heads back and taking in the gold and green and fuchsia sparks exploding over us in the form of starbursts or fantastic down-raining flowers.

Here I sigh. That last sentence just doesn't come anywhere close to evoking the actual visual or auditory experience. Not to mention the smell of burnt powder and drifting smoke picking up a little salt and seaweed tang, mingling with the annoying cigarette of the man next to me. Or my awareness that the colors overhead were complicated by a peripheral sense that the intense light of the launching rockets had lit up the water a peculiar army-surplus green, while a cheerful little blue and yellow inflatable skiff to our right rocked on the wavelets beneath all that celestial action.

But what struck me most was this: as the bits of fire came arcing down, they streaked across the night at the same time that I became aware of the spider-smoke behind them, strange contrails and patterns left where the flares had been; these were already shifted and lengthened by the wind—so that, beneath the descending display of lights, a kind of ghost display moved at a right angle to the first, strangely, like a visible history of fire written on the night.

That is a lot to try to fit into words, and it has taken me a paragraph to note, somewhat awkwardly, what the eye took in in a fraction of a second. I tried to put it into a single sentence in order to suggest, as Proust did, the simultaneity of perception. He wanted to dilate the sentence toward its outer limit, so that one would feel the blur of space and time that the unit of syntax held all at once, as it were—like seeing a whole landscape reflected back to you in a single drop of water. Because I'm not him, the attempt to render visual intricacy makes words feel unwieldy, like sacks of meaning that must be lugged into place, dragged here and there, then still don't feel quite accurate.

Which raises the question, why bother? Is it necessary to render this bit of perception into words? Why do I feel compelled to get this right?

To try to explain this feels a little like peering down my own throat in the mirror, trying to see inside myself. Hopeless. It's what I do, the nature of my attention, the signature of my selfhood: finding the words. When my friend Lucie took a lot of luggage on a trip, her host looked at her askance and said, *All that's yours?* Lucie drew herself up and said, *That's the kind of person I am.* And that was the end of that. They had arrived at an understanding.

But of course I can't leave it at that. What is it about the representation of the sensory world that compels so, what is the character of this desire?

It *is* a desire, an immediate impulse in the face of wonder or pleasure or feeling confounded or flummoxed. A need that flares up, as if it were my work in the world to do exactly this. To find accurate words, or, more ambitiously, terms commensurate with the clamoring world. Walt Whitman makes a myth of it in "Out of the Cradle Endlessly Rocking" when he traces his own origin as a poet to the boyhood experience of hearing the song of a solitary bird beside the Long Island shore. The bird had lost his mate and sang into her absence, but the boy who overheard him felt somehow required to answer, to make a song in response to the rhythmic outpouring of longing offered to him:

> Demon or bird! (said the boy's soul,)
> Is it indeed toward your mate you sing? or is it really
>   to me?
> For I, that was a child, my tongue's use sleeping,
>   now I have heard you,
> Now in a moment I know what I am for, I awake,
> And already a thousand singers, a thousand songs,
>   clearer, louder and more sorrowful than
>   yours,
> A thousand warbling echoes have started to life
>   within me . . .

The moment described is the originating point of a haunting, a felt imperative so commanding as to constitute a kind of possession. He who's awake with a thousand songs cannot stop singing.

But of course the song of the poet differs from the pure sonic outrush of the bird in that it's also an act of naming. (Just what birds are actually up to when they sing isn't clear, but it seems unlikely that they are doing what we think of as "naming" things.) The song that Whitman sings back to the migrating warbler describes the bird and its situation, describes the experience of listening beside the sea, describes the sea itself as a "fierce old mother" whose constant iteration is the whispered word *death*. Whitman's song, then, holds up a mirror to our mortal situation. As perhaps the bird's does, too, but who can say?

What we want when we describe is surely complex: To solve the problem of speechlessness, which is a state without agency, so that we feel impressed upon by things but unable to push back at them? To refuse silence, so that experience will not go unspoken? To be accurate (but to what? the look of things, the feel of being here? to the strange fact of being in the face of death?)? To arrive at exactitude in order to experience the satisfaction of matching words to the world, in order to give those words to someone else, or even just to savor them for ourselves? Critical theory is full of discussion of the inadequacies of speech, and it's true that words are arbitrary things, assigned to their objects in slippery ways, and that we cannot rely on words to convey to another person what it is like to be ourselves. "What proof do we have," writes Craig Morgan Teicher, "that / when I say *mouse,* you do not think / of a stop sign?"

But we have nothing else, and when words are tuned to their highest ability, deployed with the strengths the most accomplished poets bring to bear on the project of saying what's here before us—well, it is possible to feel, at least for a moment, language clicking into place, into a relation with the world that feels seamless and inevitable. If that is a dream, so be it. At that instant when language seems to match experience, some rift is healed, some rupture momentarily salved in what Hart Crane called "the silken skilled transmemberment of song."

What a word, *transmemberment:* it suggests the exchange of body parts, one being fusing with another, a Latinate gloss on Shakespeare's "sea change." I think of it as a kind of fusion between the word and the world, one becoming—at least in one "floating instant," to paraphrase Crane—a part of the other, grown indistinguishable.

The need to translate experience into something resembling adequate language is the writer's blessing or the writer's disease, depending on your point of view. That's why Whitman isn't sure if what sings to him is a demon or a bird. If it is indeed a symptom of a problem, of life not having been really lived until it is narrated, at least that's a condition that winds up giving real gifts to others. The pleasure of recognizing a described world is no small thing.

A Tremendous Fish

"That's *exactly* how it happened," Elizabeth Bishop said nearly thirty years after her poem "The Fish" was written. "I did catch it just as the poem says. That was in 1938. Oh, but I did change one thing; the poem says he had five hooks hanging from his mouth, but actually he only had three. I think it improved the poem when I made that change."

Talk about a fastidious sense of accuracy! But this emphasis on precision is a little misleading; the interviewer transcribed Bishop's comment with the emphasis on *exactly*, but her poem is actually more concerned with exactly *how* it happened. Here's the poem:

The Fish

I caught a tremendous fish
and held him beside the boat
half out of water, with my hook
fast in a corner of his mouth.
He didn't fight.
He hadn't fought at all.
He hung a grunting weight,
battered and venerable

and homely. Here and there
his brown skin hung in strips
like ancient wallpaper,
and its pattern of darker brown
was like wallpaper:
shapes like full-blown roses
stained and lost through age.
He was speckled with barnacles,
fine rosettes of lime,
and infested
with tiny white sea-lice,
and underneath two or three
rags of green weed hung down.
While his gills were breathing in
the terrible oxygen
—the frightening gills,
fresh and crisp with blood,
that can cut so badly—
I thought of the coarse white flesh
packed in like feathers,
the big bones and the little bones,
the dramatic reds and blacks
of his shiny entrails,
and the pink swim-bladder
like a big peony.
I looked into his eyes
which were far larger than mine

but shallower, and yellowed,
the irises backed and packed
with tarnished tinfoil
seen through the lenses
of old scratched isinglass.
They shifted a little, but not
to return my stare.
—It was more like the tipping
of an object toward the light.
I admired his sullen face,
the mechanism of his jaw,
and then I saw
that from his lower lip
—if you could call it a lip—
grim, wet, and weaponlike,
hung five old pieces of fish-line,
or four and a wire leader
with the swivel still attached,
with all their five big hooks
grown firmly in his mouth.
A green line, frayed at the end
where he broke it, two heavier lines,
and a fine black thread
still crimped from the strain and snap
when it broke and he got away.
Like medals with their ribbons
frayed and wavering,

a five-haired beard of wisdom
trailing from his aching jaw.
I stared and stared
and victory filled up
the little rented boat,
from the pool of bilge
where oil had spread a rainbow
around the rusted engine
to the bailer rusted orange,
the sun-cracked thwarts,
the oarlocks on their strings,
the gunnels—until everything
was rainbow, rainbow, rainbow!
And I let the fish go.

"The Fish" continues a tradition of seeking, in the vast book of difference the American continent offers, opportunities to be educated. The poem interprets a wordless, creaturely presence—like Whitman's "noise-less patient spider" or Emily Dickinson's "narrow fellow in the grass"—and provides, in its way, speech for that which is wordless. "Every object rightly seen," wrote Emerson, "unlocks a new faculty of the soul." The poet turns to the natural world, pays close attention, and is rewarded with instruction. The news this particular fish carries is the possibility of endurance; he's an exemplar of survival—even victory—in the face of struggle. How could such a "battered and venerable" old soldier not serve as a heroic example?

But if this were the poem's sole intent, it could have been much shorter. Instead of getting to the point, Bishop is concerned with the experience of observing; her aim is to track the pathways of scrutiny. Elsewhere, she praises "baroque sermons (Donne's, for instance)" that "attempted to dramatize the mind in action rather than in repose." That's precisely what's going on in this poem: a carefully rendered model of an engaged mind at work.

First she notes sound and weight, fusing impressions synesthetically in a startling phrase, "a grunting weight." Peeling scales provoke simile: the fish's surface is reminiscent of the condition and pattern of ruined wallpaper. There's pleasure taken in working out this comparison, and these lines signal just how leisurely and careful an examination this will be. The poet seems to proceed from a faith that the refinement of observation is an inherently satisfying activity. To see is joy and scruple, privilege and duty. No wonder she loved Vermeer!

Now the poem's structural scaffolding is established: a shuttling of attention from outward detail to inward association, mind moving swiftly from observation to reverie. The eye moves restlessly over the surface of the fish, as if seeking what might satisfy it. The "camera" roves, pans, lingers, moves in for an extreme close-up, fixes a moment on the pulsing of the gills:

> While his gills were breathing in
> the terrible oxygen
> —the frightening gills,
> fresh and crisp with blood,
> that can cut so badly—
> I thought of the coarse white flesh
> packed in like feathers,
> the big bones and the little bones,
> the dramatic reds and blacks
> of his shiny entrails,
> and the pink swim-bladder
> like a big peony.

Within this single sentence Bishop travels from fish body to human body and back to fish flesh again, entering deeply into what is literally the fish's inner life, the hidden stuff of flesh and bone. It's a painterly passage, with its arrangement of white flesh, "dramatic" reds and blacks, and the image of that startling flower-pink bladder hurrying us back to land, to some remembered garden, to the shape and sheen of a peony blossom.

The eleven lines that follow—about those haunting, yellowed eyes, with their scratchy shine—are the most extended and intricate of the poem's descriptive acts so far, as if to focus our sights on the primacy of vision here, dilate our attention, and slow our movement forward. You can't help but think about the speaker's eyes, too, and the poet points attention this way carefully: "seen through the lenses," "to return my stare." Progress slows even further when the first of Bishop's characteristic hesitations is introduced:

> —It was more like the tipping
> of an object toward the light.

That little pause and gathering of breath—just a dash, followed by the careful qualifying phrase "It was more like"—makes a world of difference. What does it mean, for a poet to stop and consider, to question herself, just as she will again in a few lines at "—if you could call it a lip"?

This hesitation reveals that what's been stated so far isn't necessarily authoritative; each descriptive act is one attempt to render the world, subject to revision. Perception is provisional; it gropes, considers, hypothesizes. *Saying* is now a problematic act, not a given; one might name what one sees this way, but there's also that one, and that one. And if we're not certain what we should say, can we be certain what we've seen? A degree of self-consciousness, of uncertainty has entered the project of description.

This reflexive awareness enters the poem just at its moment of maximum strangeness, as the speaker tries to look into those shifting eyes that can't be comfortably anthropomorphized. They don't "return my stare," and seem more like objects than like part of a living thing. And though the speaker has tried, as is her wont, to connect them to the familiar through similes, it doesn't work; you can feel, in that hesitation, and in the close study of this alien gaze, the thrum of anxiety.

No wonder, after such a moment, that the speaker begins to seize on a meaning for what she sees, a means of interpretation. This old soldier's war wounds ("like medals with their ribbons / frayed and wavering") occupy so many lines because it's here the speaker has seized on a way of "reading" the exemplar of strangeness she holds before her. She begins to claim him as a hero, attaching the poem's gathered perceptions to a sense of meaning. Though it's enormously to the poem's credit that not all of her observations can be marshaled to support this "point." There's no necessary relation between "the pink swim-bladder / like a big peony" or those unsettling eyes and the fish's ability to persist through adversity. A lesser poet might have edited out the material that doesn't conform to the message. But the wealth of detail keeps the fish from becoming a symbol and allows it to remain creaturely, its inscrutability intact even as the poem offers us an interpretive act.

Every achieved poem inscribes a perceptual signature in the world. Bishop's work of seeing offers, ultimately, a precise portrayal of the one who's doing the looking. Here stands a specific, idiosyncratic sensibility. A poem is a voiceprint; someone in particular speaks, and becomes, in the most accomplished poems, unmistakable.

You don't need to know a thing about the poet's life or circumstances. We can only guess why she might be concerned with defeat and victory, or with survival. It isn't for us to know whatever hooks she herself may bear. Instead, we're brought into intimate proximity to the slipstream of her sensations. Subjectivity is made of such detail, of all the ways in which the world impresses itself upon us, known through our associations and histories, our scaffoldings of concerns and interests, the tones and shadings of our moods. We're invited to form a sort of readerly alliance with Bishop's speaker, brought close to what she's feeling and seeing at a moment of intense clarity. Poetry concretizes the singular, unrepeatable moment; it hammers out of speech a form for how it feels to be oneself.

"How it feels to be oneself" has a great deal to do with the experience of time. It's oddly difficult to describe what subjective time feels like. The clock on the wall simply ticks, persisting in its steady progression, while those in the body and psyche call for a great variety of verbs to describe less readily chartable motions. The time of interiority pools, constricts, tumbles, and speeds. We live in a felt narrative progression, through which experience is transformed into memory. And memory edits its records of the past like a brilliant *auteur*—cutting, juxtaposing, creating a pace determined by the direction and emotion of a story. What is memory but a story about how we have lived? In Virginia Woolf's *To the Lighthouse* it takes dozens of pages to render the inner lives of a group of people sitting around a dinner table during a single meal; later in the book, decades pass in a few pages. This kind of shifting feels accurate because it replicates something of our internal sense of time, where the irrelevant portions blur while significant moments swell.

But there is another sort of temporality, too, which is timelessness. In this lyric time we cease to be aware of forward movement; lyric is concerned neither with the impingement of the past nor with anticipation of events to come. It represents instead a slipping out of story and into something still more fluid, less linear: the interior landscape of reverie. This sense of time originates in childhood, before the conception of causality and the solidifying of our temporal sense into an orderly sort of progression.

Such a state of mind is "lyric" not because it is musical (though the representation of these states of mind usually is) but because we are seized by a moment that suddenly seems edgeless, unbounded. The parts of a narrative are contiguous, each connecting to the previous instant and the next, but the lyric moment is isolate. Though it most often seems to begin in concentration, in wholly giving oneself over to experiencing an object, such a state leads toward an unpointed awareness, a free-floating sense of self detached from context, agency, and lines of action. Bishop herself described this sort of attention in a famous letter to Anne Stevenson: "What one seems to want in art, in experiencing it, is the same thing that is necessary for its creation, a self-forgetful, perfectly useless concentration."

Self-forgetful concentration is precisely what happens in the artistic process—an absorption in the moment, a pouring of the self into the now. We are, as Dickinson says, "without the date, like Consciousness or Immortality." That is what artistic work and child's play have in common; both, at their fullest, are experiences of being lost in the present, entirely occupied.

There are, in essence, only seven lines of narrative in "The Fish." The first six occur right at the beginning, bringing us into the scene:

> I caught a tremendous fish
> and held him beside the boat
> half out of water, with my hook
> fast in a corner of his mouth.
> He didn't fight.
> He hadn't fought at all.

These lines are extremely plainspoken. The verbs are simple, the last two sentences clipped off with firmly placed, line-ending periods. Of these facts, we might infer, there can be no doubt; they are the "objective" layer of the poem, its outer skin. The stuff of casual narration, their style is answered by the equally blunt final line, "And I let the fish go."

Everything else in this poem behaves differently. The remaining sixty-nine lines are concerned with the inside of the story, attention freely drifting between fish and an interior territory of association, reflection, imagination, and interpretation. Since the fish is, after all, "tremendous," the speaker can't be holding him "half out of water" for very long; this encounter must be a very brief one. But the moment dilates as it is described, creating an alternate sense of duration. It's like one of those Japanese paper flowers Proust mentions in the Overture to his novel, the kind locked up in a seashell; drop it in water and out blooms something that you'd never think could be contained in something so small. Looking and looking causes time to open; sustained attention allows us to tumble right out of progression.

How long does it take, exactly, to stare into the eyes of a fish? His eyes are

> . . . far larger than mine
> but shallower, and yellowed,
> the irises backed and packed
> with tarnished tinfoil
> seen through the lenses
> of old scratched isinglass.

Here's a beautiful series of echoes. Sometimes it's simply the chiming of a repeated vowel (*far* and *larger, scratched* and *glass*); sometimes it's a more complete rhyme (*shallow* and *yellow, backed* and *packed*). Then there are echoed initial consonants (*tarnished* and *tinfoil*), and subtle groups of near-rhymes (*seen* and *lenses* and *isinglass*). Such music-making lends the surface of language the complexity and interest of the surface that's being observed. The tongue and the muscles of the jaw must work to produce these sounds; even when we're reading silently there's a subtle physical participation taking place, an unspoken sounding of the poem's words. This physicality—heightened by a progression of sounds whose thickness means we have to labor to enunciate them—is a way of mirroring the physicality of the world.

It also, of course, takes time. It's a slightly longer activity, sounding a line like "the irises backed and packed," than it is to speak a plainer line like "I looked into his eyes." On a subtle level, this variation speeds the poem up and slows it down again, allowing our movement through the lines to mimic the character of experienced time.

Bishop slows time further by delivering "The Fish" in short lines, some as brief as two or three words. This makes for lots of interruption of the movement of the sentence. Each of the three longest ones—the gill description, the evocation of the pierced jaw, and the transformation of the boat into a location of prismatic color—takes up eleven lines, and thus each is interrupted ten times by a bit of silence or white space. Momentum is slowed by these constant, carefully placed visual delays. And there's no rest here between stanzas, simply one long flow of little units of perception; the absence of stanza breaks suggests seamlessness; our attention's suspended.

Why, if the poem is out to shift time and put us inside a scene of altered awareness, has the poet chosen to use the past tense? An experimental recasting suggests the answer:

> I catch a tremendous fish
> and hold him beside the boat
> half out of water, with my hook.
> He doesn't fight.
> He hasn't fought at all.
> He hangs a grunting weight . . .

This fails to convince. The present tense asserts that all this is being seen in the now, and that the poem's a straightforward record of perception. But a reader feels intuitively that this isn't so. The process cannot be this complete or leisurely as it is happening.

Instead, the examination of the fish is happening again in the composition of the poem, in a second layer of time. This "second layer" is the contemplative dimension of recollection—meditative but dynamic, penetrating deeply into the fish's body, rigorously attending to the peculiar character of its gaze. Perhaps the experience of joy the poem chronicles, in the final lines, was the character of the original event ("that's *exactly* how it happened"). But surely the understanding of that joy, the interpretive work that holds the sources of such feeling to the light, is the work that has gone on at the desk, where the dimensions of being open themselves to investigation. The poem's a work of inquiry—or at least a compelling replica of such a process, designed to enlist the reader's participation in a version of the work of consciousness.

Bishop tells us this event was in the past, then writes with such immediacy and vivacity as to deny us any sense of distance, and all the poem's speeding up and slowing down suggests she's out to play with time. In this light, her ending's a small stroke of genius. We read the final line as past tense consistent with the body of the poem: I let the fish go yesterday, or last week, or years ago. But since *let* is also the present-tense form of the verb, the line also has the immediacy of something happening now, as if the poem's final gesture of release is still taking place.

When she thinks of that stained rose wallpaper, our speaker's attention has left the here and now; she's no longer in the boat but in some other room, a landscape of memory or of daydream. She's begun to slip the confines of the body, moving freely in time and space. Later, as she thinks of the "dramatic" landscape inside the fish's body, she seems to have slipped out of herself, for a moment, to imaginatively penetrate the alien form. Studying the fish's eyes again leads her to a highly specific association—the eyes of an old stuffed animal? the scratched isinglass of some Victorian child's toy? Bishop doesn't stop at the cornea but seems to come right up to the retinal backing of the eye, with its tarnished shine. In and out, from one to the other, until the speaker's boundaries blur.

When the speaker in "The Fish" knows the fish's jaw is "aching," and when she perceives "wisdom" in his beard, she's entered into the fish's life. It's this blurring that prepares us, as the speaker stares and stares, for the poem's leap toward transcendence.

This fish may be a consummate survivor, but a heroic example isn't enough to make the world before one seem filled with "rainbow, rainbow, rainbow!" We feel that way when we loose our boundaries in time, no longer imprisoned by the external narrative of chronology. People slip out of the story they're living all the time; daily life is full of small moments of rupture, disappearance, and interiority. But sometimes these experiences are more lasting, and more profound. The woman in the boat holding her catch has floated out of causality; her encounter with otherness restructures her sense of the world.

Why should it be an animal presence that provokes happiness? Like the moose that engenders an experience of joy in another of Bishop's poems, the fish may be a metaphor, but it can't be *just* that. It remains charged with fascination, refusing to be subordinated to a point. Its strangeness persists, both as and after it is interpreted.

It must be in part the wordlessness of creatures. Our speech rushes in where there are no words, and in the process we understand that our acts of description are both bridges to animal life and evidence of our distance from them. The very tool we reach for to approach them holds us at bay.

"The fish," Nicholson Baker says of this poem in his novel *The Anthologist,* "doesn't want to be described." Baker's reading of the poem—or should I say his character's take on it?—is dazzling: those lines hanging from the fish's jaw are lines of poetry, "all the many other attempts to rhyme this old fish into poetry." The fish must be released, he suggests, because "you have to return reality to itself after you've struggled to make a poem out of it. . . . It needs to breathe in its own world and not be examined too long."

When our imaginations meet a mind decidedly not like ours, our own nature is suddenly called into question. We place our own eye beside that of the fish in order to question our own seeing. Consciousness can't be taken for granted when there are, plainly, varieties of awareness. The result is an intoxicating uncertainty. And that is a relief, is it not, to acknowledge that we do not after all know what a self is? A corrective to human arrogance, to the numbing certainty that puts a soul to sleep. It's the unsayability of what being is that drives the poet to speak and to speak, to make versions of the world, understanding their inevitable incompletion, the impossibility of circumscribing the unreadable thing living is. Perhaps the dream of lyric poetry is not just to represent states of mind, but to actually provoke them in the reader. Bishop's poems restore us to a sense of energized, liberating uncertainty.

But there, I try to explain why the presence of the fish and the moose provokes joy and reinvigorates the self, and all I do is place another construct of language beside the speechless fact of the other. Baker has it right, "you have to return reality to itself." The body of the fish, the moose's hairy flanks elide certainty, refuse elucidation, blur the relationship between then and now, I and you. And they persist—if people allow them to—as presences that instruct and resist us at once.

Remembered Stars

What descriptions—or good ones, anyway—actually describe then is consciousness, the mind playing over the world of matter, finding there a glass various and lustrous enough to reflect back the complexities of the self that's doing the looking.

Here, for example, is the Metaphysical poet Henry Vaughan, opening a poem called "To His Books":

Bright books! the perspectives to our weak sights,
The clear projections of discerning lights,
Burning and shining thoughts, man's posthume day,
The track of fled souls, and their Milky Way,
The dead alive and busy . . .

To use an exclamation—*Bright books!*—as the opening phrase of a poem is an energetic gesture; it promises that the following lines will, with equal élan, unpack that phrase, teaching us to read its implications. *Bright* is certainly not the first adjective that comes to mind when we think of printed volumes. Though of course the poet's process is irrecoverable, I'm willing to bet that it was this phrase that came first, in a sort of (forgive me) flash. It's a familiar experience to poets, that arrival of a phrase laden with more sense than we can immediately discern, a cluster of words that seems to know, as it were, more than we do.

In the lines that follow you can feel the muscular progression of Vaughan's thinking: books are bright because they provide lights to our dim vision, and because they clearly project a lantern light that might help us discern our way in the world, or make difficult choices when it's hard for us to see the right ones. But they're bright too because of the incandescent energy of thinking and creating, the blaze of consciousness that has been inscribed upon those pages. And suddenly it's as if Vaughan recognizes that since, in these volumes, thinking is no longer contained within the time-bound human body, it outlasts us, to become our "posthume day." How lovely the notion that the light of books is the day of the afterlife, that a *made* sunlight shines past the grave.

But it's the next, breathtaking line that wildly enlarges the poem's scale; "the track of fled souls, and their Milky Way" makes these books a shining streak across the firmament, and invites us to consider the stars themselves as evidence of human passing, the still-burning traces of consciousness gone. We've traveled from library to cosmos in a flash, and in the process what has been lost to us is suddenly restored to life, in an unexpected resurrection. Here is how Susan Howe puts it, three hundred-odd years later:

I wished to speak a word for libraries as places of freedom and wildness. Often walking alone in the stacks, surounded by raw material paper afterlife, my spirits were shaken by the great ingathering of titles and languages. . . . While I like to think I write for the dead, I also take my life as a poet from their lips, their vocalisms, their breath.

Description is a mode of thinking; in generating appositives for "bright books," Vaughan unfolds a metaphysic, an argument against the apparent erasures of our mortal condition. It's a startlingly non-Christian afterlife. Do you want to live forever? Write! But I joke—in reality Vaughan is the most Christian of poets, though a subversive one, and he offers the afterlife of the book here as a kind of emblem, evidence of a faith in the soul's persistence so deep that even the stars themselves might be seen as *our* lights.

George Herbert's "Prayer" is structured in a similar fashion; the poem's composed of a list of appositives or metaphorical equivalents for its title. In a sense it is nothing but a chain of descriptive phrases, but what a work of thinking and naming takes place here, an almost physically palpable process of argument as the poet works his way through a complicated notion of what praying is:

PRAYER the Churches banquet, Angels age,
   God's breath in man returning to his birth,
   The soul in paraphrase, heart in pilgrimage,
The Christian plummet sounding heav'n and earth;

Engine against th' Almightie, sinner's towre,
   Reversed thunder, Christ-side-piercing spear,
   The six daies world-transposing in an houre,
A kinde of tune, which all things heare and fear ;

Softnesse, and peace, and joy, and love, and blisse,
   Exalted Manna, gladnesse of the best,
   Heaven in ordinarie, man well drest,
The milkie way, the bird of Paradise,

Church-bells beyond the stars heard, the souls bloud,
The land of spices, something understood.

Herbert simply suppresses the verb (Prayer *is* . . .) and
proceeds with a supple chain of definitions of prayer. It
is one of the most beautiful modes of description, this
catalog of names; it's the mode of the litany, a way of
accumulating terms of praise.

But a list, as readers who have waded through some
of Whitman's less candescent moments know, can easily grow numbing. Herbert makes his accumulation of
descriptive phrases a dynamic, forward-moving thing,
one that includes evidence of struggle. This is espe-

cially clear in the second stanza, which startles after the trumpet praise of stanza one. It's only when we come to "Engine against th' Almightie, sinner's towre" that we're pushed back to the verb in the previous line: prayer is a swift mode of traversing heaven and earth, and its "plummet" leads into the depths of the stanza to follow. It's extraordinary to think of railing at God— using words as engines of war, building a tower in order to thunder back at the old thunderer—as prayer. But to include that kind of outpouring as also being a form of colloquy with God widens Herbert's poem, enlarging his discussion of what it is to commune with the divine.

A few lines later, here's the Milky Way again, now a part of what is surely one of the lovelier lists in the language. This bead string of phrases is energized by its variety of tone, its surprising mixture of nouns, and a lush sensory engagement in what is primarily an emotional and intellectual process—so that prayer brings with it the sound of bells, the scent of spices, the sharp tang of blood.

It's unexpected, after all the poem's sensory precision and clarity of expression, Herbert's arrival at that final phrase: "something understood." *Something* in lesser hands might seem vague and general, but here the nature of this understanding must be left open, undefined, because it's the sum of all that has transpired across four stanzas of attempts to evoke prayer's complex character. We arrive at an indeterminate term that contains all that's come before and something else too, the language-resistant stuff of internal comprehension, the intuition of grace—here phrased, most tellingly for this poet, as "understanding." Herbert doesn't want to just *feel* holiness; he values the active work of understanding. It's as if we've climbed a ladder of phrases, each in its shifting register of tone and associations, to arrive at this final rung, which turns out to be the simplest one of all, on the surface of it, but from which language can climb no higher.

In Gerard Manley Hopkins's breathless sonnet "The Starlight Night," a still more conflicted, wilder worshipper turns his attention to the heavens:

> LOOK at the stars! look, look up at the skies!
> O look at all the fire-folk sitting in the air!
> The bright boroughs, the circle-citadels there!
> Down in dim woods the diamond delves! the elves'-eyes!
> The grey lawns cold where gold, where quickgold lies!
> Wind-beat whitebeam! airy abeles set on a flare!
> Flake-doves sent floating forth at a farmyard scare!
> Ah well! it is all a purchase, all is a prize.
>
> Buy then! bid then!—What?—Prayer, patience, alms, vows.
> Look, look: a May-mess, like on orchard boughs!
>   Look! March-bloom, like on mealed-with-yellow sallows!

These are indeed the barn; withindoors house
The shocks. This piece-bright paling shuts the spouse
Christ home, Christ and his mother and all his hallows.

Hopkins seems madly in love with the surface of the world here, the night sky dazzle. His opening injunction repeats the same verb three times: *look, look, look*, as if to suggest that no one's ever seen such a marvel. He offers us six lines of ecstatic description, figure upon figure flung back as if in answer to the splendor. They're curiously pagan images for a Jesuit poet *(fire-folk, circle-citadels, elves'-eyes)*, tinged with a sense of the Celtic myth world whose twilight the young Yeats will sing a few decades hence. Hopkins filled his notebooks with precise observations of the natural world, and probably the trees that enter the poem—whitebeams, abeles (another name for white poplars)—come right out of his daily walks; these are both trees whose leaves have whitish undersides, and in a breeze they're spangled with white. The visual experience of their flashing, unsettled leaves seems to lead the poet directly to the next, unlikely image. How unlikely, and lovely, to think of stars as resembling scared birds flying up in a farmyard when a door or gate is opened! That scattter seems to lend the stars a sound as well as movement, and these birds are made all the stranger by being "flake-doves"—tiny, easily stirred by the least motion, sparks or bits of ash blown up from a blaze.

Just when it seems this dazzle of descriptors can't be sustained another moment, Hopkins breaks his stride. "Ah well!" seems to suggest it's impossible to continue, that none of these tropes can do the work the poet requires. What can be said save that it's *all* desirable, all a prize to be won, but how can we own the world, how come to possess it? What do we have for currency to bid in the grand razzle-dazzle auction of starlight? Four one-word terms, the priest offers us: *prayer, patience, alms, vows.*

But just when the poem seems to set its course in the direction of spiritual advice, the celebrant of the world (who here, as elsewhere in Hopkins's poems, struggles to reconcile the delights of earth with the demands of heaven) once more takes the stage and turns his attention upward.

I wonder if there's another sonnet in English that uses the same verb seven times? *Look, look,* this passage begins, as if whatever the speaker might have said in the previous, rhetorical lines is entirely overwhelmed by physical reality. "May-mess, like on orchard boughs" provokes in me a state of happiness that makes critical discussion practically impossible. I'll try: there's the marvelous tension between the rest of the line and the entirely unexpected "mess," as fine an example of polarity in descriptive speech as I can think of. There's the alliterative pleasure of "May-mess," a poetic device that seems to come from the same ancient realm of Britons as do the four trees the poem catalogs. There's the pleasure of being told twice in this line to *look* at the marvelous parallel messes of orchard and stars, a doubling that intensifies our sense of the speaker's character, his enthusiasm, his giddy pleasure in being overcome by what is, for him, the sensory evidence of the divine. We're given one more tree, willows with their yellow early-spring catkins, and then the sonnet moves to its startling close. That farmyard back in line seven must still be lingering in Hopkins's imagination, because it seems to lead toward the figure that provides the poet with his idiosyncratic revisioning of all the glories he's been cataloging as—a barn? The stars in all their spangled fire are a barn to house the divine, merely the outer "piece-bright paling" that contains the true glory?

"Piece-bright paling" requires a bit of unpacking. *Paling* is a row of upright, pointed sticks—a picket fence. When we repeat the familiar phrase that something is "beyond the pale," we're employing what Donald Hall has called a dead metaphor, using a comparison we don't even notice anymore because it's become a cliché or because the vehicle it employs to make meaning has lost its significance in contemporary speech. "Beyond the pale" means to go outside the fence, though I doubt there's a living speaker of English who thinks of a fence as "a pale."

"Piece-bright" suggests first the individual pickets, all agleam in their white paint, the shining enclosure of the heavenly host. But "piece-bright," Paul Mariani writes, is also a term for money, taking us back to the poem's middle lines about buying and bidding, and Hopkins must want us to hear the homonym "peace-bright" too. "Paling" also suggests the fading of the stars, at dawn, as the Son appears in the final line, and it also suggests that the stars themselves must pale beside the divinity they house. (It still seems odd, and deeply engaging, that Christ must here be figured as a sort of animal, since he dwells in the barn. Are we to think of the site of the Nativity? Or to think of him as some transforming beast?)

The stars themselves may pale, but it's instructive to notice that they still get nine lines of this poem, lines sparked by eleven exclamation points! If the stars are merely the farm building in which the Hallows reside, it's abundantly clear that this poet truly loves the barn.

Here is one more starry example of description as an active process of thinking. "Voyages," Hart Crane's great sequence, traces the course of an ecstatic union between two lovers. One is at sea, moving through "adagios of islands," while the poem's speaker bridges the distance between them with a potent metaphoric re-creation of their passion—a total immersion in which the transmembering power of the sea brings them to an orgasmic moment when "sleep, death, desire, / Close round one instant in one floating flower."

In section V, a crisis arises. The two seem to be together again, perhaps back on the Brooklyn rooftop of Crane's apartment building, looking out toward the East River and the harbor, where "the bay estuaries fleck the hard sky limits." And that hardness seems to have inflected and informed them; their intimacy has been compromised or diminished by some "piracy." Now, Crane says, with his trademark density:

> The cables of our sleep so swiftly filed,
> Already hang, shred ends from remembered stars . . .

Though the poet does not mention Brooklyn, no reader of Crane can encounter these lines, especially after the poem has located us with what seems a splendid evocation of New York Harbor in winter, without hearing in those hanging cables an evocation of the bridge, which he elsewhere calls "harp and altar."

The bridge's cables seem to narrow as they descend, as if they'd been filed to sharper points, and if you've seen the bridge in fog it wouldn't be at all unlikely to think of those hanging cables as "shred ends." But these are the cables "of our sleep," which seems to suggest a bridge between the lovers, or lines of connection binding them. Cables that hang in shred ends support nothing, of course; our mutual sleep is lost now. Since the context of the poem is nautical, and the beloved's been away at sea, "cables" also suggests messages sent from shore to ship and back again, missives telegraphed between them. Such communiqués might be filed away, as old love letters sometimes are, no longer read, but too lovely or painful to discard. And what's left now? Shred ends—of the nocturnal, wordless bonds, of the ties between them, of the bridge that might lead them toward one another or into the future—hanging from what can no longer be seen, the lights of heaven that can only be remembered, no longer useful for navigation, no longer guiding them forward.

Crane thinks, here, through description, twining strands of meaning, braiding together elements of his thinking and perception to make an image both elusive and unforgettable. He would, I think, agree with the notion that such imagery comes closer to being commensurate with reality than ordinary speech. Its density melds perception with thinking and feeling, making a new, generative reality: the poetic image alive in its multiplicity of meanings, unparaphrasable.

Instruction and Resistance

It's incomplete to say that description describes consciousness; it's more like a balance between terms, saying what *you* see and saying what you *see*. The seer of Concord, in the dictum I've quoted previouly, insists that it's not just looking at things that reveals the self, but vigilant, careful seeing: "Every object rightly seen unlocks a new faculty of the soul." The more accurate and sensory the apparent evocation of things, the more we have the sense of someone there doing the looking, a sensibility at work. It's as if the harder the eyes and the verbal faculties work to render the look of things, the more we see that gaze itself, the more we hear that distinctive voice. Shelley's handwriting, wrote his friend Trelawny, "might have been taken for a sketch of a marsh overgrown with bulrushes, and the blots for wild ducks." How true to marshes, true to a messy hand in ink, revealing of the man who's looking at both and making the seamless connection between them.

Sometimes only a little sense perception is enough to become the vehicle for a great deal of thinking and feeling. Here is Rilke's famous auto-epitaph, in Stephen Mitchell's translation: "Rose, oh pure contradiction, joy / of being No-one's sleep, under so / many lids." To point to the resemblance between petals and eyelids is one thing, a form of visual accuracy, but to suggest what lies beneath those lids is to enter into the inner life of the rose, into the subtler dimensions of the way that flower means within the inner life of the speaker. So many eyelids over no one's sleeping—is there a comment there about collectivity, the way the world's body is held in common, belonging to no one? Or does "no one" point toward an absence at the heart of the world, a phantom presence felt through emptiness? Or we can read the image as pointing to the way that roses seem entirely, permanently awake, and call us toward the same sort of alert being.

E. M. Forster described the great Alexandrian poet Constantin Cavafy as "a Greek gentleman in a straw hat, standing absolutely motionless at a slight angle to the universe." There in a very few words is a movement from the particular to the immense, balancing the least detail (a straw hat) with the great field of being. Forster invites us to consider all the ways in which one might stand "at a slight angle" to that field.

Or there was the Japanese philosopher—I regret that I don't know his or her name—who said, "A fish never makes an aesthetic mistake." That is a statement, on the one hand, a rhetorical move, but it sends us hurrying to every visual image of fish we can think of, to see if it could be true. It describes a notion of beauty, a way of valuing the effortless, the uncalculated, the unwilled.

Since there is so little sensory evidence in these examples, they seem to be diving beneath, attempting to name some elusive quality of their subject. They name the object of their attention without in the least depriving it of any of its mystery. They instruct us in what is here to be seen, and they resist too easy a knowing.

This quality of resistance is an aspect of the most resonant of descriptions. How does it happen that an evocation of the sensory world also suggests the limitations of such evoking, maintaining a sort of open space? Rilke, Forster, and that philosopher whose identity I cannot discover each create a space of indeterminacy, a kind of field—circumscribed by their precise sketch of their subject—in which meaning isn't closed or completed, but remains instead generative. When Baker says "the fish doesn't want to be described," he points toward this unresolvable, and therefore energizing, zone in which what we say about things can't ever be conclusive.

One of the twentieth century's most forceful examples of this principle is also one of its best-known poems, Ezra Pound's inexhaustible "In a Station of the Metro":

The apparition of these faces in the crowd;
Petals on a wet, black bough.

The poem is so quick and compressed that it operates on us before we've even had time to think about what's happening; it's as if the subway doors have been flung open in Times Square and there you are, immersed in a human world that's both immediate and immense. There's a slight internal gasp that comes with that experience: oh, I was in a contained space, and suddenly it's opened into a vast one. Pound's poem describes the Métro in Paris, but the grand spaces of public transportation, the big hubs of coming-and-going, are signature spaces of international modernity. In train stations, subway stations, airports, bus stations, we're lifted out of our individual focus into the stream of people in motion—and there are so many of them, in London or Paris, Barcelona or D.C., all plucked for a moment out of context, become bits of light in the great pouring stream of being on the way to somewhere.

Because it's such a tiny poem, merely fourteen words (plus six for a title that does the useful work of placing us specifically, so that the body of the poem can turn its attention to the heart of the matter), it's instructive to consider the contribution that these tremendously pressurized terms are making to the whole.

Apparition comes with connotations of color, so that the faces seem pallid, even transparent. More important, it establishes a tone for the visual image to come, suggesting that the speaker's haunted, that perhaps there's a sort of unreality, a phantom quality to the suddenly appearing strangers, and a heightened sense of subjectivity. Imagine the poem as "These faces in the crowd: / Petals on a wet, black bough." That would make a claim about what reality is, and the poem becomes descriptive in the less profound sense of the term—simply an evocation of the look of things. *Apparition,* though, makes the poem a description of the speaker's reality, the world-as-it-is-being-known-and-felt. *Apparition* is the poem's secret source of energy; without the word, the memorable resonance of this poem—its lonely, beautiful ache—vanishes.

These faces—not *those,* or *some,* or even just plain *faces.* The modifier brings the speaker into a more dynamic, immediate relation to the people before him; these particular faces loom. *The crowd* on the other hand is more distanced; it doesn't feel the same as *this crowd* would, and lends a sense of distance to the speaker's relation to the undifferentiated mass.

Petals, by nature, tend to be small, and thinking about small petals against the big black background of the Métro station makes the individual human seem tiny, and perhaps suggests something about the speaker's sense of the weight or proportion of an individual life. What are *petals* now were flowers once; a wholeness has been shattered. The image pulls us in two directions at once: the faces, like petals, have been separated from an original unity, losing their structural connection, yet there's also a sense here of a continuum of life, a kind of human brightness. The human face is what blooms, renews, and shines in the dark. Perhaps it's raining, and the assembled mass in their soaked slickers have the look of a "wet, black" branch. The sight of these individuals (are they?) in the urban dark, their faces made brighter against the dark shine around them, is chilling and disconnected, but you can also read it as an affirmation. The poem won't let us have it one way or another, finally.

I don't want to leave Pound's poem without pointing to the perfection of that semicolon. Imagine replacing it with words:

> The apparition of these faces in the crowd
> . . . is like petals on a wet, black bough
> . . . reminds me of petals on a wet, black bough
> . . . resembles petals . . .

Enough! But these awful distortions of the poem point to how much life is in that little double jot of ink, with its power to suggest but not define linkage. With nothing but the punctuation mark between the poem's elements, we experience the disparate nature of these two things more intensely. The more yoked things do not have in common, the greater the level of tension, the greater the sense of cognitive dissonance for the reader. We have to work in the poem, and we feel something happen, instantaneously, in the yoking of those faces and those petals. The use of *like* here would have drawn a firm line between the two elements, but without such a firm gesture of equivalence we confront a metaphor that is far more alive in its associations, far more ambiguous, and more crucial.

An image, Pound wrote, "is that which presents an intellectual and emotional complex in an instant of time. . . . It is the presentation of such a 'complex' instantaneously which gives that sense of sudden liberation . . . which we experience in the presence of the greatest works of art. It is better to present one Image in a lifetime than to produce voluminous works." (Something he might have kept in mind later on.)

An instantaneous intellectual and emotional complex is precisely what we get in this poem. And how deeply satisfying it turns out to be that we can't quite finish mining the poem for its conjoined intellectual and emotional content. It seems both an evocation of alienation and a recognition of commonality; tonally, it seems composed of equal portions of sorrow and wonder. Pound's poem stays with us because it yokes unlike things, allows us space to move, and refuses to make a direct statement, forcing us to remain in the position of interpreter of something that is perpetually open.

Four Sunflowers

William Blake's sunflower, the best known of its tribe in English poetry, appears in a poem that has almost nothing about it that is conventionally "descriptive":

Ah, Sun-flower! weary of time,
Who countest the steps of the Sun,
Seeking after that sweet golden clime
Where the traveller's journey is done:

Where the Youth pined away with desire,
And the pale Virgin shrouded in snow
Arise from their graves, and aspire
Where my Sun-flower wishes to go.

This sunflower is less individual than emblem, employed here for Blake's metaphysical and intellectual purpose. Only one characteristic of the flower, its phototropism, is onstage, the flowerhead held high in seeming longing for a golden realm it can't reach. But Blake wouldn't be the great poet he is if he could allow his bloom to be entirely symbol. Those first two lines give us some of the physicality of this bloom, a quality most evident in the choice of verb in line two. Many two-syllable verbs might have worked here—*mirrors, follows, shadows, studies, markest*—but *countest* is splendid in both content and sonic effect. To follow or emulate those steps is one thing, but to actually count them—now there is a wearisome project. How many steps must be required to traverse the heavens? "Countest" is a little hard to say, especially when placed beside the echoing *st* in *steps.* The subtle difficulty of negotiating these sounds echoes how hard the sunflower's work is, how it labors at its devotion.

You are reading Blake's poem without the aid of his designs for the page, which change the experience of reading his *Songs of Innocence and Experience,* from which this poem is drawn. But the hand of Blake the painter and engraver is nonetheless evident in the way that the first three lines of the second stanza are entirely pale and wan, after *sunflower, sun,* and *golden,* which together create a warm blaze of yellow in the opening stanza. The energy and vitality of that hue drain away, in the next stanza, in the colorless evocation of the pining youth and the chill of *pale, shrouded,* and *snow.* It's only in the last line that color returns, and it's accompanied by one of Blake's masterfully subtle moves: it's no longer *a* sunflower, or *the* sunflower, articles that have been implicit in the poem's opening lines, but instead a bloom attached to the speaker, who himself becomes visible to us at this last, telling moment.

My sunflower means multiply: That the flower blooms in Blake's own yard, both literally and in his garden of emblems. That the sort of aspiration embodied by this flower's relentless devotion to heaven is not foreign to him; has he himself practiced, or is he in danger of, such attention to some "sweet golden clime" to come that he cannot attend to the consequences of this desire here on earth? The youth and the pale virgin are dead, vanquished by unfulfilled desire; the sunflower stands erect, at attention, as the emblem of pure longing. *My* suggests, with a hint of wit and of playfulness, that the speaker knows he's read this flower in one particular light, his own, and that other readings might also be admissible. The sunflower might be read as an emblem of loyalty to heaven, of the human thirst for a better realm—but *my* sunflower critiques this position, standing as a figure of our unanswered longings—both of sexual desire gone unfulfilled and what the poet insinuates is a substituted longing, the thirst for paradise.

Two hundred years later, Alan Shapiro's sunflower has dropped the wimpy longing for deliverance and is not in the least bit tired:

Sunflower

No pitying
"Ah" for this one,
no weariness
about it or
wanting in the
upward heave
of its furred stalk
curving and opening
out into a
cup of pointy
leaves, each leaf
alert with tiny
quills, spines,
prickles—
       did I
say *cup*
    of leaves?
Say shield instead,
say living
crucible
from which flames
burst with such
sticky brightness
that they suck
sunlight down

into the in-
fluorescent burning
pit of itself.
      Did I
say sunflower? Say,
instead, don't-ever-
mess-with-me. Say
there-is-nothing-
I-won't-do-to-live.

Blake's bloom is intent on lifting off from daily reality, dedicating itself to the quest for transcendence, but Shapiro's flower plans to make its flaming way in this world, so insistent that it requires a revision of its usual name.

The work of naming—how we are to describe what's before us—is Shapiro's clear subtext. Since the speaker's a reader of poetry, he begins with a literary reference point, an accepted, art-derived way of looking at the blazing phenomenon in front of him. But the framework of Blake's poem will not do, not when the terms this flower generates include *heave, curving, opening,* and *alert.* Shapiro's self-consciousness about how to say what's experienced, the work of finding commensurate terms, leads to the two questions that lend the poem its argumentative structure. "Did I / say *cup* / of leaves?" once again questions a more conventional perception; the flower is not a receptive thing, for which the familiar metaphor of the waiting receptacle will do; it requires instead *shield, crucible,* and *pit,* terms of a far greater ferocity. *Crucible* gives us one of the poem's only one-word lines, indicating that this may be the crux of the matter, this near-archaic word with its connotations of flame and molten metal, magical heat and transformation. It's this understanding of the sunflower as a burning crucible of transforming energy that leads to the next question: "Did I / say sunflower?" Will that term do at all, now that the given associations have been set aside and the radiant, struggling form seen as it is? Now new terms are offered, not unlike Herbert's appositives for prayer, and the sunflower's new names feel thrillingly self-generated, proudly self-chosen appellations. This bloom is so empowered that it even seems to generate the poem's form, a narrow pillar of text resembling its own body.

It's a lovely subtlety of Shapiro's poem that, even as it sets Blake to one side, there's a nod to the older poem in the new poem's ending. *Me* appears here at the last moment, just as *my* did in the earlier text. The result is that those tough-talking names feel like they belong to the speaker as well as to his flower; they're what an Alan Shapiro sunflower would say, the cry of the determined survivor.

Another twenty-first-century sunflower towers by night in a poem by Tracy Jo Barnwell. Flowering in some

urban dark, Barnwell's bloom recalls the beat-up city
sunflower in Allen Ginsberg's "Sunflower Sutra":

> . . . poised against the sunset, crackly bleak and dusty
> with the smut and smog and smoke of olden
> locomotives in its eye—
> corolla of bleary spikes pushed down and broken
> like a battered crown, seeds fallen out of its face,
> soon-to-be-toothless mouth of sunny air, sunrays
> obliterated on its hairy head like a dried wire
> spiderweb,
> leaves stuck out like arms out of the stem, gestures
> from the sawdust root, broke pieces of plaster
> fallen out of the black twigs, a dead fly in its ear,
> Unholy battered old thing you were, my sunflower
> O my soul . . .

Barnwell addresses her sunflower directly, too, but this
is a blossom that wouldn't even think of transcendence;
instead it's a member of Lord Death's troops, an assis-
tant to the disruptive powers of the night:

Night City Sunflower

Black bloom of Broadway, light's last night watchman—
you do your job grudgingly, staring down the bail
bondsman
with your one good eye.

You're full of doubt. Where's this morning they talk
    about?
For all you know this night could be the one that
    lasts.
You have the petals

of a killer, the build of a boxer. And just what
do you think you're looking at, poker face? Want
to fight, Sunflower?

How many peonies have you strangled with that
    crooked
stalk of yours? The other weeds steer clear of your
    jagged
crack in the sidewalk,

the drunken carrion crows fly to the other end
of the block to avoid the searing yellowness
of your gaze,

and the poor clover wither in your shade. Every night
owl knows you—the midnight walkers and bad sleepers,
the few shivering

passersby walking quickly under hooded coats,
the suddenly hungry heading for any of a hundred
glowing all-night

diners, the lonely shadows in their windows,
and the twitching figures pacing endlessly
from one end

of the world to the other. I've seen you from time to
    time,
leering from your deep hole in the universe.
In some field

there are thousands like you, all lined up in rows and
    rows
of yellow, each turning slowly in unison with the next,
each collapsing

in a bow of reverence for the light that passes over.
These thousands would wilt in the anemic neon gleam
    that
sustains you. *Tattoo.*

Big Love Motel. Midnight Massage. Open All Nite.
You cannot turn your face towards the sun,
but you shiver

slightly at passing headlights or the occasional star.
Who will dare to cut you down when you are frosted
    over
with snow?

I turned once to see you swaying darkly beside me—
you bowed your head slightly as I passed by.
Later, half-asleep,

I could still hear your leaves rustling like the sleeves
of a black wool coat—the coat of a preacher or a
     watchman
or a pallbearer.

Barnwell's driving, incantatory address to this flower of the night gains much of its power from an inversion of our expectations; the poem's like a photographic negative of a sunflower, where all we expect to suggest brightness and diurnal good cheer turns to its opposite. This tough-minded bloom is like some solitary trench-coated figure in an archetypal noir backstreet.

Come to think of it, all the sunflowers depicted here gain power from resisting the flower's conventional associations: Blake's flower pines, its phototropism a sign of insatiable longing. Shapiro's flames and talks tough. Ginsberg's hides illumination beneath its grimy skin, while Barnwell's lives on neon alone. They're self-portraits, at least in the sense of portraying some aspect of the speaker's psyche, and they manage to be true to sunflowers, too, in the slyest of ways: they foreground the character of the flower by insisting that we see it in some unfamiliar light, finding qualities nearly opposite to those we might expect. Poetic description wants to do anything but reinscribe the already known; if we look deeply enough into anything, is what we find the opposite of what appears at the surface? "If we had a keen vision and feeling of all ordinary human life," George Eliot wrote in *Middlemarch*, in one of those breathtaking moments when the novelist stands back from her tale and seems to take in the whole of the landscape with a sweeping eye, "it would be like hearing the grass grow and the squirrel's heart beat, and we should die of that roar which lies on the other side of silence."

Description's Alphabet

Description is an ART to the degree that it gives us not just the world but the inner life of the witness.

—————————————————————

BEAUTY is not loveliness, grace, or pleasurable sights, though any of those might certainly be part of it. For the writer out to evoke the texture of experience, beauty is simply accuracy, to come as close as we can to what seems to be the real. As Galway Kinnell writes, in perhaps the only sentence in English where the same verb repeats three times in a row and still makes sublime sense: "Whatever *what is* is is what I want."

Or as Susan Howe puts it, precisely:

> because beauty is what *is*
> What is said and what this
> *it*—it in itself insistent *is*

This morning brought Manhattan the biggest snow-storm of the year. Here a good snow is a major event; the almost unstoppable city slows, quiets, and brightens. In Washington Square dogs are rolling in drifts, children sled on tiny artificial hills, and the few shoveled paths empty into expanses of white.

But across the street, in a gallery at NYU, is a pure, concentrated area of COLOR. It's a small and engaging show of paintings Richard Diebenkorn made in Albuquerque, in the early 1950s. How do these things look so alive? Taking in these forceful squares and rectangles of intense activity, I answer that question in different ways.

Sheer push and pull of shape and line, the restless energy inherent in these masses and their dynamic relations.

This is the work of an artist in transition. He hasn't quite figured out who he is yet, how he's going to proceed, and instead of the settled mastery of the later Diebenkorn there's a restless experimentation, a trying on of different densities of paint, various surfaces, degrees of busyness and calm.

And it's 1951, and how many people in the world have any idea how to look at these bold new paintings? It's as if they've been made in secret, and their radicalism lends them a sort of urgency, a perpetual quality of surprise.

But the prime source of vitality here is Diebenkorn's absolute mastery of color, his enthrallment to hue. In his hands—or, literally, in the paint that comes through his hands—color seems to be fully what Goethe called it, "the deeds and sufferings of light."

Desert color: arroyo thunderhead stone clay ochre mud sand quartz shadow.

No literal presentation of landscape, but the paintings document an encounter with earth and sky, stone and space anyhow. Forceful striking raking desert light. Cartography. Aerial mapmaking. Inebriate's immersion, inhabitation of hue.

The writer laments ever being able to dwell in color in this way, since we can never experience written color so—well, wordlessly. Never approach that immediacy, that unmediated encounter with, say, red. How does color get onto the page, into the reader's internal eye? Certainly not by naming it; it doesn't do much to say *the red door.* Not enough there for the senses to work on, not enough specificity in the naming and not enough engagement of the other senses—which, of course, like to work in concert. As soon as I add another qualifier, a shadow of dimension appears: *the scraped red door.* Go a little further and physicality begins to materialize: *the rough, scraped red door.* Two textures have now been added to the color, and in "rough" there's even a suggestion of place—it doesn't sound domestic, or urban—and of age.

Readers may remember when every mailbox in America sported the J. Crew catalog, with its nouveau prep clothes, every T-shirt or sweater available in a range of colors with memorable names: *pool, pine, sierra, stone.* It's marketing kitsch, but those writers knew what they were doing; the word not only makes us see the color in a way that a more straightforward name never would, but also invokes an inviting world of associations, the aqua splash of *pool,* the scented cool of *pine.* It's an indirect way of naming, and it avoids the problem of color words that can seem as flat as Crayola hues, and tend to lead to lying anyway. When we refer to leaves as green or bark as brown, we reduce language to a debasing perceptual shorthand. Every leaf is made up of a complex interaction of shades, tones that shift as light does. Watch a Russian olive toss in the wind in sunlight! (Back to Hopkins's "wind-beat whitebeam" and "airy abeles.") What you see is as far from "green" as the appallingly named "flesh" of the crayon boxes of my childhood is from the beautiful variety of human skin. Even to say the phrase "Russian olive" is to bring something of the flashing, always-moving aspect of those leaves with their silvery undersides into speech, if only by association.

With that in mind, I'll add another bit of color to my imagined portal—*the rough, scraped red door beside the spruces*—and now the first color is thrown into dialogue with the shadowy black-green introduced by the word *spruces.* It's the same way a painter energizes one color by placing another beside it, cultivating opposition and tension. Denise Levertov renders a pair of colors this way:

> . . . the butteryellow glow
> in the narrow flute from which the morning-glory
> opens blue and cool on a hot morning.

Hot is such a satisfying adjective because it brings that yellow glow back onto the poem's stage, framing the cool blue of the flower with heat on either side.

A beautiful use of "oppositional color" appears in an early poem of A. R. Ammons's:

> *Winter Scene*
>
> There is now not a single
> leaf on the cherry tree:
>
> except when the jay
> plummets in, lights, and,
>
> in pure clarity, squalls:
> then every branch
>
> quivers and
> breaks out in blue leaves.

There are no cherries here, but we can't help but see a small burst of color when we hear the word, and then how rich that final *blue* becomes when it "breaks out" in the space where only a little potential red and green have been. It seems fair to say the poem's "about" the blue of winter—blue light on snow, blue winter twilights, that wintry shade in the western sky after sundown.

It's surprising how strongly the naming of particulars brings color into a poem's perceptual web. This stanza by Robert Hass arose across the continent from Ammons's poem, and uses only "silver" and "golden" as signposts to render a lushly austere summer landscape:

> The creek's silver in the sun of almost August,
> And bright dry air, and last runnels of snowmelt,
> Percolating through the roots of mountain grasses
> Vinegar weed, golden smoke, or meadow rust . . .

("That Music")

Roots and grasses, vinegar and smoke and rust: perhaps this stanza comes as close to a painting (impossible, longed-for accomplishment) as a poem can get.

People who have studied drawing know that you have little idea what's in front of you in the visual landscape until you try to represent it. To some degree, the art of description is the art of perception; what is required, in order to say what you see, is enhanced attention to that looking, and the more you look, the more information you get. CONTOUR DRAWING is a great example. It involves not merely trying to draw an individual thing but to follow outlines with your pencil. Try this now with just your eyes: look up from this page and choose a line before you, the outer edge of anything, and start to follow it; where it intersects with another line you have to choose which way to go. The resulting visual journey can feel intricate indeed; it makes us see the world before us as composed not of discrete things that don't touch, but as a continuous realm of interconnected lines.

To be better at description, we have to work at attentiveness.

Here is my horoscope, by Rob Brezsny, for the week of
Valentine's Day 2008:

Scholar Suzanne Juhasz says that Emily Dickinson's
eroticism "inflects and charges" most of her poems.
"Erotic DESIRE—sensuous, nuanced, flagrant,
extreme, outlandish, and profound—is her way of
interacting with the world." From an astrological
perspective, it would make perfect sense if you ex-
perimented with a similar predilection in the coming
days, Leo. During the superheated grace period you'll
be enjoying, interesting things are likely to happen to
you if you basically just make love to the whole world.
The urge to merge shouldn't just be the icing on the
cake. It should be the icing, the cake, the plate it's on,
your eating of the cake, your feeding of the cake to
others, and all the stories you tell yourself about your
encounter with the cake.

ECONOMY is a virtue, albeit an overrated one. No one would want Proust to have less to say about asparagus stalks, for instance, but such a fulsome discourse only works when perception itself is the subject. Proust's novel is, after all, a huge inquiry into the nature of consciousness, a magnificently nuanced evocation of what it is to see and sense. And if it *is* too much? EXCESS, which is seldom understood to be a virtue, can certainly be a pleasure.

Speaking in FIGURES

Here's one of those stories everyone swears is true, though they always seem to have happened to a friend of a friend, and are never quite verifiable. I heard it from my friend Genine, and I'm not quite sure where she got it. A man was telling his therapist about a fight he'd had with his mother. They were standing together in the kitchen, arguing, and then, he said, "My mother put the icing on the cake." The therapist said, "Oh?" "Yes," he said. "She put the icing on the cake?" "Yes." The therapist persisted: "But how did she put the icing on the cake?" "She put the icing on the cake." And so it continued, until they realized they were talking about a literal cake; the mother was holding a knife covered with buttercream frosting.

A few summers ago, in Prague, I had the opposite experience. Considerately, restaurant menus often offer English translations beneath the Czech listing, but the translations are often dodgy. "Beef consommé with faggots," for instance, took us aback, but nothing was as hard to figure out as an appetizer called "smoked language." Then one of the diners at our table decoded the dish, which was tongue.

The therapist assumes language must be metaphoric; the dogged but well-intentioned menu translator assumes it must be literal. I tell these two little bits of anecdote because they point to the absolute centrality of figurative speech. You could say that all language is metaphoric, since the word stands for the thing itself, something the word is not. In her memoir, *The Names of Things,* the Egyptologist Susan Brind Morrow points to the origins of letters in the observation of nature, how the scuttle of crab claws on sand, for instance, influenced the hieroglyph for "writing." To use words at all is to use them figuratively; we breathe metaphor, swim in metaphor, traffic in metaphor—and the verbs in those three phrases illustrate my point.

Poetry's project is to use every aspect of language to its maximum effectiveness, finding within it nuances and powers we otherwise could not hear. So the poet needs to be a supreme handler of the figurative speech we all use every day, employing language's tendency to connect like and disparate things to the richest possible effects. In poetry, figuration is at its most sophisticated: condensed, alive with meaning, pointing in multiple directions at once. And it's crucial to notice that simile and metaphor are not simply ornamental devices, like frosting on the cake of sense. Far from being just ways to make meaning seem more attractive, figurative speech itself means, and means intensely. It's one of the poet's primary tools for conveying the texture of experience, and for inquiring into experience in search of meaning.

An evocative, sexy poem by May Swenson serves as

an elegant and accomplished example of the principles
of figuration in action:

Little Lion Face

Little lion face
I stooped to pick
among the mass of thick
succulent blooms, the twice

streaked flanges of your silk
sunwheel relaxed in wide
dilation, I brought inside,
placed in a vase. Milk

of your shaggy stem
sticky on my fingers, and
your barbs hooked to my hand,
sudden stings from them

were sweet. Now I'm bold
to touch your swollen neck,
put careful lips to slick
petals, snuff up gold

pollen in your navel cup.
Still fresh before night

I leave you, dawn's appetite
to renew our glide and suck.

An hour ahead of sun
I come to find you. You're
twisted shut as a burr,
neck drooped unconscious,

an inert, limp bundle,
a furled cocoon, your
sun-streaked aureole
eclipsed and dun.

Strange feral flower asleep
with flame-ruff wilted,
all magic halted,
a drink I pour, steep

in the glass for your
undulant stem to suck.
Oh, lift your young neck,
open and expand to your

lover, hot light.
Gold corona, widen to sky.
I hold you lion in my eye
sunup until night.

Here are six principles of figurative speech.

1. *To say what we see is to speak figuratively.*

    The first project of simile and metaphor is to describe, to say what something's like. Unless we restrict ourselves to mere measurement, we cannot do so without resorting to comparison. In the hands of a poet like May Swenson these comparisons become a sensory—and sensual—universe in themselves. Just in the first two stanzas, her dandelion blossom is a miniature version of a great cat's face and a "silk sunwheel."

2. *Figures work together to form networks of sense.*

    Of course the metaphors that Swenson chooses are accurate to the look and feel of dandelions, but the relationships between these figures quickly suggest that the poet's enjoying a metaphoric game here; the act of picking the flower is standing in for something else. And just what that "something else" is becomes clear in the fourth and fifth stanzas, which describe modes of appreciation that would seem over the top for even the most avid lover of flowers!

3. *Figuration is a form of self-portraiture.*

    Swenson's poem is about picking a dandelion, and it's clearly a love poem as well. But its intense involvement in rich, descriptive speech also creates

another subject, which is the character of the perceiver. It's a kind of perceptual signature, a record
of an individual way of seeing. This is one of the
central things that poetry is: a vessel of individual-
ity, a distillation of the way one person experiences
the world, knows herself in time and in place.

4. *Metaphor introduces tension and polarity to
   language.*

The figurative often introduces rich and
unexpected language into a poem, shifting the
elements of its vocabulary. In Swenson's case,
consider "your barbs hooked to my hand, / sudden
stings from them / were sweet." "Barbs," "hooked,"
and "stings" probably wouldn't have entered into
this love poem if the vehicle of the dandelion
weren't there, and the poem's wiser and more
complex for their presence.

5. *Metaphor's distancing aspect may allow us to
   speak more freely.*

"Little Lion Face" is decidedly a poem of female
sexuality. The vehicle provides a bit of a "veil" here
that allows Swenson to explore a heated, charged
experience, one I doubt she would have inscribed
directly. (Emily Dickinson: *I need more veil.*) There
is a certain pleasure, isn't there, in pretending the
poem's only about picking a flower? A delight in
a (thin) disguise? When I discussed this poem in

a lecture in Logan, Utah, a number of Swenson's surviving relatives were present, and one took exception to my characterization of this piece as a poem of same-sex love. "That," she said, "is just how we used to play with dandelions." I felt a little bad for May, dead all these years and her family still wanted her to hush up! But I also remembered a student of mine who wept when we read this poem in class, because it was the first poem by Swenson anyone ever discussed in my student's academic experience, and a poem in which her own erotic experience felt so clearly mirrored. This is an excellent example of the way a good veil works: you can see just the veil itself, if you choose to. But if you want to, or you know how, you can read what lies beneath.

6. *Metaphor is an act of inquiry (not an expression of what we already know).*

I can't prove this, not having access to Swenson's process, but I can feel the power of the result. "Little Lion Face" has that unmistakable quality of discovery, the sort of energy generated when an idea (and a concomitant set of emotions) unfolds before the writer. Working out the relation between dandelion and lover engages the poet's imaginative energy. I can't imagine that Swenson knew, consciously, that her dandelion would propel the poem's investigation of erotic energy, withdrawal, and renewal.

In this way metaphor becomes a kind of argument, a "thinking through" of what's implied in a relation between things apparently unlike. And the reader can feel this active engagement of mind, especially because Swenson has embodied it in the thrilling sonic structures she's built. Listen to the cascade of long *o* sounds in these lines from near the end: "Oh, lift your young neck, / open and expand to your / lover, hot light. / Gold corona . . ." Those are the ohs of pleasure, but perhaps they are also the pleased exclamations of discovery: Oh, my metaphor has yielded meaning! Oh, I've made something complicated, full of feeling and tension, something almost as mysterious and alive as experience is.

GESTURE DRAWINGS

Sometimes the merest sketch, the quick gesture made in the direction of evoking the real, is the most satisfying. I always think of my mother's moment of rebellion, in a painting class, when she had just had enough of the strictures of the composed still life the teacher had assigned. She whipped out a sheet of watercolor paper and, with a Japanese ink brush, drew some running horses, each made out of the minimum number of strokes. Her work was fueled by exasperation, but even her teacher acknowledged that it was the best thing she'd ever done.

Description is fueled by HUNGER for the world, the need to taste, to name, to claim what's seen, to bring it, as Rilke would put it (in the ninth of his great elegies, the subject of which is the resurrection of the world within the perceiver), "O endlessly into ourselves." But it would be simplistic to conceive of such hunger as simply celebratory or affirmative; that is part of it, but it's very often true that what we are compelled to describe is terrible, or oppressive, or heartbreaking. Language is hungry for that, too. It wants, as it were, to eat everything. Even the falling and fading world, even misery.

Here is James Galvin, in a poem called "Grief's Aspect," sketching a mood of lonely, damp gloom:

> The cemetery is just a melancholy
> Marina and rain
> Is the tallest girl I know.

Those are desolate lines, but you can hardly read them without taking pleasure in them. It's the unexpected figure of the cemetery as a place to be moored, and the movement from those watery graves to the wry evocation of the rain. And the pleasure, too, of watching words find their way toward the clear naming of a psychological condition anybody would recognize; they speak to our hunger for a vocabulary for the whole range of feeling, even the awful parts.

Description is made both more moving and more
exact when it is acknowledged that it is inevitably IN-
COMPLETE. In Hayden Carruth's poem "No Matter
What, After All, and That Beautiful Word So," the speaker
tries to describe the power of the sound of wild geese
flying overhead, heard from inside the house:

> This was the time of their heaviest migration,
> And the wild geese for hours sounded their song
> In the night over Syracuse, near and far,
> As they circled toward Beaver Lake up beyond
> Baldwinsville. We heard them while we lay in bed
> Making love and talking, and often we lay still
> Just to listen. "What is it about that sound?"
> You said, and because I was in my customary
> Umbrage with reality I answered, "Everything
> Uncivilized," but knew right away I was wrong.

Carruth's acknowledgment of his limited, failed answer
to the question is what sets his poem in motion. An
easier version of the poem would stop with the notion
that our attraction to something that represents the
uncircumscribed, wild world explains the allure of the
geese's crying. But the speaker in this poem is restless,
and too honest with himself to settle for an easy explanation. The poem continues:

I examined my mind. In spite of our loving
I felt the pressure of the house enclosing me,
And the pressure of the neighboring houses
That seemed to move against me in the darkness,
And the pressure of the whole city, and then
The whole continent, which I saw
As the wild geese must see it, a system
Of colored lights creeping everywhere in the night.
Yes, the McDonald's on the strip outside Casper,
Wyoming (which I could indistinctly remember),
Was pressing against me. "Why permit it?"
I asked myself. "It's a dreadful civilization,
Of course, but the pressure is yours." It was true.
I listened to the sound in the sky, and I had no
Argument against myself.

It's startling here, how awareness moves outward, from the room that contained the poem's consciousness at the beginning to neighboring houses, to all of Syracuse, and then a vision of the continent seen from above, the "creeping" system of colored lights eating up the darkness. Then that awareness seems to come flying down to one particularly egregious example of the built, American world, an apparently memorable fast-food restaurant whose placement, in what used to be the wilds of the West, must have offended the speaker's soul. But the understanding that we've built an insufficient cultural landscape can't, finally, be brought back to the geese; their strange utterances seem to call to us anyway, and the poverty of our made world doesn't account for their allure.

The poem concludes with a compelling series of attempts to account for that unmistakable pull:

> The sound was unlike
> Any other, indefinable, unnameable—certainly
> Not a song, as I had called it. A kind of discourse,
> The ornithologists say, in a language unknown
> To us; a complex discourse about something
> Altogether mysterious. Yet so is the cricketing
> Of the crickets in the grass, and it is not the same.
> In the caves of Lascaux, I've heard, the Aurignacian
> Men and women took leave of the other animals, a
> trauma
> They tried to lessen by painting the animal spirits
> Upon the stone. And the geese are above our window.
> Christ, what is it about that sound? Talking in the sky,
> Bell-like words, but only remotely bell-like,
> A language of many and strange tones above us
> In the night at the change of seasons, talking unseen,
> An expressiveness—is that it? Expressiveness
> Intact and with no meaning? Yet we respond,
> Our minds make an answering, though we cannot
> Articulate it. How great the unintelligible

> Meaning! Our lost souls flying over. The talk
> Of the wild geese in the sky. It is there. It is so.

Over the course of this passage, Carruth proposes—and rejects—any number of terms for what he hears, and the result is such a potent complication of the nature of that sound I can't bring myself to write here a single word for it; I want to say instead "the _____ of the geese," and allow that space to include all the rejected terms the poet has offered us: *not a song, a kind of discourse about something altogether mysterious, talking in the sky, bell-like words, remotely bell-like, a language, many and strange tones, an expressiveness.* These efforts at speech are informed by the memory of our ancestors, those cave dwellers who felt the pain of our species' separation from the rest; a longing for a lost sense of connection lies behind this catalog of inadequate terms. It cannot be said, what the geese cries "mean," and yet they provoke us to answer; we can neither understand them nor cease to respond to their presence. The paradox is elegantly expressed here by a line break:

> . . . How great the unintelligible
> Meaning!

In the strictest sense, you could say that nothing unintelligible *is* a meaning, but the work of Carruth's poem has been to show us exactly that living paradox in the geese and in ourselves, the perception of meaning that can't be translated into any other form of speech. The geese are unintelligible, but we move across that space of the line break, that gap that logic will not bridge, and there is meaning; both terms are true at once. The whole poem, in a sense, is encapsulated in that tiny spatial movement; it leaps across a chasm between the incomprehensible and the making of meaning. But it refuses stable, easy, or permanent interpretation. The term *unintelligible* is not erased or elided, but yoked to its opposite.

Carruth's accomplishment here is to build a construct of language that acknowledges the "meanings" that live outside of words; we can point to why the goose calls move us but never quite explain it, since it calls us to a place words don't go. The power of this strategy is partly a function of the humility of the speaker, who does not presume knowledge, but involves us in his active quest for it, and takes the limits of language and understanding not as a reason for silence but as a spur to delve further.

On the edge of the bay, a tangle of washed-up eelgrass looks for all the world like very narrow tape spewed from some maddening marine cassette. I like this simile because of its JUXTAPOSITION of the natural and the artificial, which somehow has an inherent comic aspect to it. The humor may arise from the distance between the thing under examination and what it's compared to; it's a long way from the slick fragrant underwater plant to the now-antedated technology of those little plastic boxes full of magnetically remembered music. To yoke, within a single figure, the vegetal and the made, or the hard and the soft, or the tiny and the immense, is a means of bringing energy into language through the unexpected collision of elements that seem to meet only in the mind, in the framing field of thinking. Whitman uses such a yoking to describe grass:

> Or I guess it is the handkerchief of the Lord,
> A scented gift and remembrancer designedly dropped,
> Bearing the owner's name someway in the corners,
>   that we may see
> and remark, and say Whose?

That is a memorable description because it yokes the grass to something quite deliberately made, and quite deliberately dropped, in a ritual of flirtation. Whitman's

grass is not only an intentionally woven cloth but also
a means through which God intends to seduce us. And
the image further startles because of its shift of scale,
moving from the Lord of creation to the tiny embroi-
dered monogram on the corner of a lost handkerchief.
The metaphor holds a little further shock, too, since
the Lord's behaving in a way not usually ascribed to His
understood gender; what would America in 1855 have
made of a fellow who dropped monogrammed, per-
fumed handkerchiefs, hoping they'd be found? I suspect
he'd have been considered what Whitman elsewhere
calls a "foo-foo," even more archly, an "affettuoso."

Lynda Hull considers a spring morning in Chicago:

> ... Deep
> in last night's vast factory, the secret
> wheels that crank the blue machinery
>
> of weather bestowed this sudden cool,
> the lake misting my morning walk, this
> vacant lot lavish with iris—saffron,
>
> indigo, bearded and striated, a shock
> of lavender clouds among shattered brick
> like cumulus that sail the tops of high-rises
>
> clear evenings.

Weather here has come from a hidden industrial source, the sky's deep machinery, but this descriptive flourish isn't merely fanciful. Hull goes on linking the given and the made, like those ruined bricks atop the buildings that themselves resemble sailing cumulus clouds. A decidedly urban soul, she isn't much interested in nature apart from us; instead, she's out to confound the difference between these categories, to make the human landscape inseparable from the world. And the poem—"Chiffon," it's called—goes on to blur other categories, too: poor girls make themselves fabulous by singing in secondhand gowns; a white girl makes herself black, at least while she's pretending to be a Supreme; and the "piercing ambrosial" iris blurs the distance between now and then, between this moment and that one, between sweet memory and the bitter turns of history.

And here is Malena Mörling, evoking the dead with elegant economy, in the opening stanza of "Traveling":

Like streetlights
still lit
past dawn,
the dead
stare at us
from the framed
photographs.

Glowing past their time, the dead don't exactly illumi-
nate the present, as streetlights don't show the way after
daybreak. But lit streetlamps and the dead are presences
nonetheless, and the yoking of these two unlikely elements does an enormous amount of work in Mörling's
poem.

In each of these instances, the yoking of disparate
elements makes more than a vivid account of perception; the best description is never merely decorative, but
makes meaning in itself, building an argument about the
nature of the real.

What is veracity in description? It must be fidelity to the truth of perception—that is, attention and allegiance to a process of KNOWING. Our knowledge of the sensory world is nothing fixed, but a continuing reappraisal, a set of processes that figure and refigure the world. If the work of description is a close rendering of the process of knowing, then idiosyncratic representation is as true as anything in a more familiar mode. Poetry, after all, delights in the unexpected, and is out to refresh our eyes and ears. It's art's work, as the Russian critic Viktor Shklovsky asserted, to defamiliarize reality. To defamiliarize is quite another thing than to ignore or replace; in Shklovsky's formulation, art's work is to return us to the processes of perception and awaken us to the shifting and perennially challenging nature of what's in front of us.

So E. E. Cummings's famous "r-p-o-p-h-e-s-s-a-g-r" has little interest in the conventions of syntax, of the sentence, or of conventionally rendered detail, yet it manages to represent the action of perceiving that leaping insect with an energetic attentiveness:

<pre>
                    r-p-o-p-h-e-s-s-a-g-r
             who
        a)s w(e loo)k
        upnowgath
                PPEGORHRASS
</pre>

                        eringint(o-

aThe):l

        cΛ

            !p:

S   a

                    (r

rIvInG   .gRrEaPsPhOs)

                                            to

rea(be)rran(com)gi(e)ngly

,grasshopper;

This is like the experience of watching something leap, a sudden event happening so quickly we don't have a name for what we see, cannot identify the motion, and then, ah! it comes to rest, and the word presents itself as the sense of the poem clicks into place in the final line. It's a little drama of experiential flux, and it's only in returning to the scrambled elements that bring us to the conclusion that we can begin to sort them out. You can track and unscramble Cummings's words, but it's clear that he wants them in a stubborn suspension, not quite parsable, till we get to that marvelous interleaving of "rearrangingly" and "become" in the next-to-last line. That's what the elements of the world do, simultaneously rearrange and become, so that the event that can be seen takes place. In this way "r-p-o-p-h-e-s-s-a-g-r" might be read as a poem embodying the worldview of twentieth-century physics, with its emphasis not on solidity but on motion, the patterning life of energy, waving its way into the world of forms. It's just the right gesture for this poem to end on a semicolon; even though we've finally arrived at a recognizable, solid word, that mark of punctuation tells us the sentence is not complete, the grasshopper is soon to leap again, and the world will return to a state of process.

May Swenson might have had Cummings's poem in mind when she made her visual/linguistic version of wave motion, a remarkably precise study of a breaking tide:

How Everything Happens
(Based on a study of the Wave)

<pre>
                                    happen.
                             to
                           up
                      stacking
                        is
               something
       When nothing is happening
       When it happens
                  something
                       pulls
                           back
                             not
</pre>

                              to
                                happen.

When   has happened.
        pulling back   stacking up
                happens

            has happened   stacks up.
When it   something   nothing
                    pulls back while

Then nothing is happening.

                                    happens.
                              and
                        forward
                    pushes
                up
            stacks
        something
Then

Swenson's title makes explicit what's suggested in Cummings's poem, that the particular object being studied is representative of the larger actions of the world.
Swenson's model of waves—the intricacy of which I
further discover here by typing out the poem, a complex

exercise that makes one contemplate the up and down, the back and forth, the pull and break of waving—points to the world's ways of happening, the energetic push and pull of a world that's always coming into being. It not only defamiliarizes the break and recede of a wave, but also makes one look again at sentences and lines too, at the movement of words on a page, the ways in which we expect to read, and the way the world doesn't necessarily want to be ordered into the linearity and forwardness of text.

(Interesting to consider, too, that these two poems are made possible by the technology of their moment; hard to imagine either of them being composed in longhand. Their complicated patterning seems to require the typewriter's fluidity of spacing, and its tendency to distance the word from the hand. The dominant technology of writing in the twentieth century influences here a stance toward the positioning of words and letters, and a freedom in the deployment of white space on the page. No typewriter = no *Paterson,* no *Cantos,* no *Maximus.* There's an interesting parlor game: what great twentieth-century poems could have been written in longhand? *Life Studies,* certainly, and *Ariel.* The implications of twenty-first-century technology for poetic form remain an open question.)

Since the inadequacy of LANGUAGE is fast becoming a cliché of postmodern writing, we may have to think about how to negotiate the inescapable limitations of words without relying on a suddenly familiar hesitation, a doubt in language's capabilities. Back in the mid-90s, my students at Iowa used to like to say, "I mistrust language." Now everybody in creation mistrusts language, and half the poems we read make a nod toward the unsayable. What's to be done? Language won't do what we wish it would, but we have nothing else—so we have to go forward and behave as if it could do what we wanted (with some faith in the miraculous fact that it does, from time to time, give us a "Song of Myself" or a *Tender Buttons,* something the world wouldn't be the same without). Perhaps we can inhabit the interesting middle ground that lies between, on the one side, giving up on referentiality altogether, and, on the other, cleaving to an outdated notion that words can be controlled, can say what we mean to say when we wish to make use of them.

Don't go in fear of that which has been looked at again and again. Poets return to the MOON immemorially; it is deeply compelling and we probably won't ever get done with it. The challenge is to look at the familiar without the expected scaffolding of seeing, and the payoff is that such a gaze feels enormously rewarding; it wakes us up, when the old verities are dusted off, the tired approaches set aside.

Shelley's classic description of the moon, probably the best known in English, astonishes with its extensions:

> Art thou pale for weariness
> Of climbing heaven and gazing on the earth,
> Wandering companionless
> Among the stars that have a different birth,—
> And ever changing, like a joyless eye
> That finds no object worth its constancy?

Those first two lines alone establish a thesis, offering an explanation for lunar pallor. But the two following lines complicate the picture by pointing to the moon's solitude and lack of kinship with the stars. Shelley nervily extends his consideration even further, by proposing a cause for the moon's inconstancy, comparing it to the gaze of the depressed or the disenchanted, who find no value in the objects of perception. Thus in six lines the poet has accounted for the moon's color, its movement, and its shape-shifting, each originating in that disconsolate solitude. Shelley, as one accustomed to wandering and a sense of standing apart, would naturally understand that as the cause of the moon's behavior. Though when these lines were written in 1820 Shelley had lost his first wife, his children by her, his daughter, and his sister-in-law, and John Keats was dying in Rome. Is it any wonder then to see in the sky a "joyless eye"?

Mina Loy's moon, somewhere in the neighborhood of a hundred years later, is an object of invocation, a potential agent of liberation:

> Face of the skies
> preside
> over our wonder.
>
> Florescent
> truant of heaven
> draw us under . . .

> *("Moreover, the Moon")*

How far from Shelley's sorrow, this rebellious desire to be pulled by a "florescent truant"! Loy's choice of preposition is masterful; to be drawn "under" by the moon is go down into trouble and longing, to be swept down into an alluring tide.

The title of Brenda Hillman's late-twentieth-century poem is crucial to her figuration of the moon:

—So the moon came up
      pink tonight
like one of what had been missed

("Male Nipples")

And thus the moon becomes intimate, smallish, and a character in an erotic drama, although not a central one.

Perhaps the signal characteristic of contemporary moons is that they have lost their icy grandeur, their sense of either a sorrowful distance (as in Shelley) or an anarchic, inspiring aspect (as in Loy). Brenda Shaughnessy's moon is something of a mess:

    Your face
regularly sliced up by the moving

frames of car windows. Your light is drawn,
quartered, your dreams are stolen.

You change shape and turn away,
letting night solve all night's problems alone.

("I'm Over the Moon")

Dorianne Laux's moon might be the most unmistakably contemporary of these, evoked in a heroic (and wrenching) simile developed across the length of a single sentence some twenty-six lines long, at the conclusion of her poem "Facts about the Moon":

> These nights
> I harbor a secret pity for the moon, rolling
> around alone in space without
> her milky planet, her only love, a mother
> who's lost a child, a bad child,
> a greedy child or maybe a grown boy
> who's murdered and raped, a mother
> can't help it, she loves that boy
> anyway, and in spite of herself
> she misses him, and if you sit beside her
> on the padded hospital bench
> outside the door to his room you can't not
> take her hand, listen to her while she
> weeps, telling you how sweet he was,
> how blue his eyes, and you know she's only
> romanticizing, that she's conveniently
> forgotten the bruises and booze,
> the stolen car, the day he ripped
> the phones from the walls, and you want
> to slap her back to sanity, remind her

of the truth: he was a leech, a fuckup,
a little shit, and you almost do
until she lifts her pale puffy face, her eyes
two craters, and then you can't help it
either, you know love when you see it,
you can feel its lunar strength, its brutal pull.

Is there a MORALITY of description? If so it lies in refusal, in that which the writer will not diminish by the
attempt to supply words. Pablo Neruda, in "I Explain
a Few Things," gives witness to the destruction of a
Spanish community by fascists during the Spanish civil
war, but balks at description. The poem's best-known
lines, here in Mark Eisner's translation, are

> and through the streets the blood of children
> ran simply, like children's blood.

To make a figure of speech for the unbearable would
feel transgressive, diminishing. Nothing can be commensurate, Neruda's anti-simile seems to suggest, and
therefore nothing can be placed into that space of like-
ness, not as an equivalent of the lost lives of children.

There's a similar, moving strategy in a recent poem
of Wislawa Szymborska's, here translated from the Polish
by Clare Cavanagh and Stanislaw Baranczak:

Photograph from September 11

> They jumped from the burning floors—
> one, two, a few more,
> higher, lower.

The photographer halted them in life,
and now keeps them
above the earth toward the earth.

Each is still complete,
with a particular face
and blood well hidden.

There's enough time
for hair to come loose,
for keys and coins
to fall from pockets.

They're still within the air's reach,
within the compass of places
that have just now opened.

I can do only two things for them—
describe this flight
and not add a last line.

Szymborska's poem ends on a note of generosity and respect. By refusing to conclude the poem, she grants the falling their suspension, their last dignity, so that they remain "complete" and "particular," their "blood well hidden." Nor will she point to how deeply the speaker feels about the fate of the falling. She refuses to write a neatly concluded poem that will inevitably fall short of the dreadful subject it contemplates.

But her refusal contains a telling contradiction; despite her wish not to end the poem, she will "describe this flight." Thus her final stanza embodies the dilemma and work of the witness. How do we say what we have seen of the suffering of others responsibly? Not to respond at all is a failure, to respond too easily a lie.

A disagreement: a few years ago Yusef Komunyakaa and I were on a panel with the broad title "Poetry and the Earth." I can't remember which of us spoke first, but here's the substance of our positions: Yusef said that language comes between us and things, and that as soon as we had NAMES for what we saw, we experienced a certain degree of removal from the world. Thus, in Eden, appeared the serpent of divisive consciousness; if we could remove ourselves from kinship through the agency of language, then we could wreak havoc upon the world without feeling that we harmed ourselves.

I said that the more we can name what we're seeing, the more language we have for it, the less likely we are to destroy it. If you look at the field beside the road and you see merely the generic "meadow," you're less likely to care if it's bulldozed for a strip mall than you are if you know that those tall, flat-leaved spires are milkweed, upon which the monarchs have flown two thousand miles to feed, or if you can name sailor's breeches and purslane, lamb's-quarter, or the big umbels of wild carrot feeding the small multitudes. Isn't the world larger and more valuable, if you know what an umbel is? Thus, in Eden, paradise became a more intricate place, artfully arrayed, and its loss was felt all the more sharply.

We're both right.

Theodore Roethke: "When is description mere? NEVER."

Polarity, the pull of forces in OPPOSITION to one another, makes writing feel alive, because it feels more like
life to us than any singular focus does; reality, we understand, is a field in which more than one attraction, more
than one strong tug, is always at work. The best descriptions acknowledge the dual nature of the world, the
shading that exists at the edge of any brightness, the joke
waiting in mortality's dimmest clutch; Galway Kinnell
writes, "On the blued flesh, when it is / laid out, see if you
can find / the one flea which is laughing."

This afternoon there are two deer hanging out in
front of my garden gate. One has a particularly dull
look to her face, as if the wheels of thinking turn very
slowly indeed; the other, poor thing, has a useless hind
leg that she drags along beside her as she walks, splayed
out, no hoof at its tip. They seem like fire-sale deer, the
last ones left, the ones no one wants to take home. But
there they are, scrounging around together, not alone,
and when I brought them some carrots they ate them
with transparent relish, the one with the bad leg clos-
ing her eyes while she chewed, moving her lower jaw
back and forth in the way deer do, all pleasure.

PROJECTION: that psychological mechanism by which we turn the world, or other people—or deer—into versions of ourselves. I may have just done exactly that. For literary describers, projection is not only no sin but our stock-in-trade, our method of operating, our modus operandi, a signature of our art. The insights of modern physics—that the observer changes the observed, the measurer influences what is measured—makes what used to be called the "pathetic fallacy" seem a negative term for the inevitable perceptual work of the human. If you're miserable, then the trees look miserable to you, too; there may not be any way around this, but it's probably good to know you're doing it.

Wanting to make the world on the page seem real to the reader, our first impulse is sometimes to reach for adjectives and adverbs, those QUALIFIERS intended to lend a host of sensory qualities to the sentence or the line. But be careful; it's often the case that writers turn to those additives—like spices in the kitchen—when the main ingredients themselves seem bland. If the nouns and verbs themselves aren't interesting enough, no amount of adjectival or adverbial flavoring is going to really do the trick.

Thus this exercise: from a draft in progress, remove every adjective and adverb, and see what you've got left. Can you strengthen any of the nouns and verbs remaining, through greater specificity or precision? To illustrate my point, consider the difference between *tree* and *sassafras*, between *tool* and *adze*. You can't say *sassafras* when you mean *tree*, but often there's a more exact term waiting to be employed.

Now, which, if indeed any, of the qualifiers you've erased do you really miss, which ones are absolutely necessary?

It isn't my intention to advocate for severity. I love Louise Glück's poems, with their severe economy of means, but the more maximal Alice Fulton's allusive, shimmery surfaces delight as well. Style, as Jean Cocteau said, is a simple way of saying complex things. What is said, by style, is something about a view of the world, and about the work of poetry itself, and about the speaking character of the poet, who's introducing us to a personal mode of knowing, a private language as various as human character is.

Still and all, I think of my late partner, a window designer with an infallible ability to make anything look great, who used to repeat a bit of fashion advice: after you're dressed, go to the mirror before you go out and take off one accessory.

If I were asked to say what distinguishes an artistic temperament from any other, I'd say that it's a fundamental sense that the project of being alive is something peculiar, little understood. I've always felt amazed by—a bit envious of—people who take their lives for granted, who feel that of course *this* (this body, this community, this set of human laws and social expectations) is the way things should be, how could it be otherwise?

But to believe that the world is QUEER, or that oneself is, or both, is a window of doubt through which all creative possibility comes into being. I'll return to Forster's description of Cavafy as "a Greek gentleman in a straw hat, standing absolutely motionless at a slight angle to the universe." That "slight angle" is of course homosexuality, as it was for Forster himself, but that's just one aspect of a kind of oblique position in relation to the real, one that is often enabled by sexual difference but in no way restricted to it. That "absolutely motionless" has something to tell us about Cavafy's peculiar position in time. Cavafy was also a person to whom the ancient world was remarkably vivid; he's said to have gossiped about figures of the Hellenic world of old Alexandria with as much avidity as he might talk about his peers. He apparently did not much care if his mother knew he was a lover of men, but was careful to conceal from her the fact that he was a poet. Which is the queerer trait?

In this American moment, it's fundamentally queer to be a poet, queer to be interested in what can't be packaged or sold in the marketplace, queer to enjoy the fundamentally useless, contemplative pleasure of poetry. Queer means that which is not business as usual, not solid identities founded on firm grounds, but a world in question.

Not everything can be described, nor need be. The choice of what to evoke, to make any scene seem REAL to the reader, is a crucial one. It might be just those few elements that create both familiarity (what would make, say, a beach feel like a beach?) and surprise (what would rescue that scene from the generic, providing the particular evidence of specificity?).

The musicality of poetry, its SONIC texture, is a value in itself. It is, to some degree, the essence of poetry, that which makes the poem irreplaceable by a straight-forward translation into prose: the poem's body of sound is its specific, particular flesh.

But sonic texture also has a particular role to play in the work of description, which has to do with making represented reality feel more convincing to us, making language more markedly like the world. Here's a passage from Gary Snyder's *Myths and Texts:*

> Stone-flake and salmon.
> The pure, sweet, straight-splitting
>   with a ping
> Red cedar of the thick coast valleys
> Shake-blanks on the mashed ferns
>   the charred logs
> Fireweed and bees
> An old burn, by new alder
> Creek on smooth stones,
> Back there a Tarheel logger farm.
> (High country fir still hunched in snow)

Snyder's first line gives us two nouns held together by *and;* the work of the sentence is the yoking of these two elements, which might be said to be representatives of a landscape, signature elements of a place. Because they're yoked, we're invited to think about the relation of flakes to fish scales, of the gray of stone to the gray-pink-mica-granite of salmon flesh, and there's some suggestion of the animate and the inorganic as one thing, one conjoined body. Two *s*'s, one long *a* and one short one, two *l*'s, that short-line music clipped by the sudden period at line's end.

Then a big, rambling, airy sentence opens out, as if we've turned from the precise examination of one bit of detail to the wider scene on the trail ahead, a landscape made out of consonants and vowels. The lines beg to be read aloud; mouthing them, you can't help but feel the knotty interruption of forward momentum in "The pure, sweet, straight-splitting / with a ping / Red cedar of the thick coast valleys." "With a ping" even gets indented on its own line, to make the movement knottier; the cedar splits straight but it's resistant too, and the lines echo the fragrant density of the wood and the nice solid ring it makes splitting apart under the ax.

I don't know exactly what a "shake-blank" is, though it must be related to cedar shakes, the shingles cut from cedar logs. But the line has such a firm physical reality to it that I want to relish "shake-blanks on the mashed ferns" as a passage of muscular motion involving tongue and jaw: the two hard *k*'s ending the first words echoed by the *d* and *f* later on, the long *a* in the first word giv-

ing way to the two chiming short ones of *blanks* and
mashed. Every one of the six words in the line is a mono-
syllable, which makes this chain of sound seem harder,
rougher.

And so it goes. We proceed along Snyder's lines as
though they were themselves a trail, a pathway through
a wood of sounds, an unmistakably specific landscape,
the poet fiercely loyal to the local.

Allegiance to locality sings also in "Kosmos," in which
Yusef Komunyakaa addresses Walt Whitman. This
passage is from a section of the poem contemplating
New Orleans, a city home for a time to Whitman and
to Komunyakaa himself:

> Wind-jostled foliage—a scherzo,
> a bellydancer adorned in bells.
> A mulatto moon halved into yesterday
> & tomorrow, some balustrade
>
> full-bloomed.

The landscape here, as much cultural as physical, is
lush, sensuous, flowering. Music arises not only from
what's named, that scherzo and jingle of wind-tossed
leaves, but also from the cascade of *l*'s *(jostled, belly-
dancer, bells, mulatto, halved, balustrade)* and the internal rhymes *(scherzo/mulatto, halved/balustrade, moon/*

bloomed). This is an enrapturing city, redolent of history and of eros, and the poem's act of elaboration signals the speaker's desire to immerse himself, to be back there, in an ecstastic engagement in memory.

Sonic texture can itself be a form of praise, a kind of savoring of things. When Galway Kinnell speaks of "the long, perfect loveliness of sow" he wants us to feel the mouth-resonance of those *o*'s—*long, love, sow*—elongating the *o* in *long,* holding it against the shorter *o* of *love,* then the deeper vibration of *sow,* so that the soughing and roundness of the vowels themselves become a kind of parallel text to the creature herself, stating an emotional position toward her, physically fulfilling or demonstrating the pleasure and blessing the poem describes.

―――――――――――――――――――――――

Here is Frank O'Hara on a particularly subtle sound:

> Vaguely I hear the purple roar of the torn-down
>   Third Avenue El
> it sways slightly but firmly like a hand or a golden-
>   downed thigh

What a skein of complicated perception has been delivered to us there in a casual but very economical pair of lines! This is the opening movement of a poem titled "You Are Gorgeous and I'm Coming," and encountering these lines immediately after the title suggests that vague violet roar is an approximation of the sound of approaching orgasm, if you could hear the onrush of that bodily event, unstoppable as an approaching train. And it's made more bodily by the sway of hand and thigh—the occasions of that sexual excitement?—and the way that thigh's golden fleece glows in such painterly opposition to the purple of the remembered roar of the oncoming train.

The result is something like a snapshot of the image-making mind at work; train and thigh, hand and roar, the superimposition of both events and of senses—all these serve to make a representation of consciousness.

SYNESTHESIA, the blurring of the senses, suggests that the senses are separate, and that crossing the boundaries between them is a sort of literary technique, when in fact there's little boundary between, say, tasting and smelling, and sight and sound and touch fuse together every moment to form the sensorium, the sphere of perception in which we dwell. What's odd is the convention of separating sense perceptions, as if we knew one in isolation from the others—when in fact I'd suggest that it's actually work to sort them out, to try to experience, say, pure sound. O'Hara's two lines are brilliant because they're such an accurate rendering of an idiosyncratic process of sensory overlap and association. The writer who wants to come closer to the lived texture of experience could do no better than to allow the senses their complexly interactive life.

Every gesture contributes toward the establishment of TONE. James Galvin's "Special Effects" opens with a description of laundry:

> My shirts on the line
> (One sleeve has fondly blown
> Around its neighbor's shoulders)
> Look like drunks at a funeral.

Though seemingly effortless, this image defines the emotional position of the speaker. The image is comically mordant, because the comparison isn't just to inebriates but to sodden guys at a funeral. And that single adverb, *fondly,* does a lot of work; something about it demonstrates the speaker's wryness. He's evoking a moment of gloom, but he's also able to stand back and take some pleasure in this descriptive act, or at least to lightly mock his own sardonic stance, so that there's a characteristic quality of brio to this darkness.

Tonal work like this provides vividly rendered information about the character and state of mind of a speaker. Here's a telling example from James L. White's "Making Love to Myself":

> After work when you'd come in and
> turn the TV off and sit on the edge of the bed,

    filling the room with gasoline smell from your
        overalls,
    trying not to wake me which you always did.
    I'd breathe out long and say,
    'Hi Jess, you tired baby?'
    You'd say not so bad and rub my belly,
    not after me really, just being sweet,
    and I always thought I'd die a little
    because you smelt like burnt leaves or woodsmoke.

The lost beloved is recalled through a remembered scent, the most physical and immediate of the senses. *Gasoline, burnt leaves,* and *woodsmoke* work together to build a world around the "you," who seems to be a working-class man, someone who works outdoors perhaps, who wears the same uniform to work every day. There's no way to predict that penultimate rhetorical line, with its intense statement of feeling, or that it will lead into a concretely descriptive one. It's a little shock, going from death to overalls, in a way that must be like what the speaker feels putting his face to that fabric and inhaling that fragrance. The simple gesture of putting these details in the past tense—*smelt* and *I always thought*—places the relationship firmly in the past, so the sense perceptions noted become sharply elegiac, a flash of memory that hasn't lost its immediacy. We're conscious, too, of the speaker's vulnerability, the way his outcry of feeling plays against the earthiness of the line that follows it. Finally, you can't help but feel the echo of the poem's title in "die a little," a nod to the Elizabethan sense of orgasm as a little death, when the soul left the body for a moment. The speaker in this poem is trying, unsuccessfully it seems, to move toward that conclusion himself, but he keeps getting sidetracked by grief. The intoxicant smell of those old overalls is both aphrodisiac and a chastening reminder of what can't be held again.

UNCERTAINTY

Questions are always a little more trustworthy than answers. And even if what is said does not take the rhetorical form of a question, the best descriptions contain room for that which must remain indeterminate; they somehow manage to acknowledge the fact of limit. John Ashbery turns to his convex mirror for "as much brisk vacancy as is to be / my portion this time." A. R. Ammons concludes his walk on "Corsons Inlet":

> enjoying the freedom that
> Scope eludes my grasp, that there is no finality of vision,
> that I have perceived nothing completely,
>   that tomorrow a new walk is a new walk.

We don't always need the poet to tell us "I have perceived nothing completely," but we want to feel that pressure, that quality of both eagerness and humility, pushing toward the boundary and acknowledging that the boundary is there.

The descriptive force of the right VERB is enormous; it bears a kind of muscular concreteness, making the written world seem dynamically present. Here are some apt, hardworking verbs from three recent poems.

Michael Dumanis ventriloquizes the artist Joseph Cornell addressing one of his own creations:

> You are the obligation, Box, to harbor
> each disarray and ghost.

Harbor is a striking choice, there, since it suggests safety and shelter at the same time that it suggests the subversive act of harboring a criminal. It's not a verb you'd expect to be used with these particular objects, but to assert that what Cornell's orderly boxes do is to harbor disarray and ghosts feels exactly right; they resist disorder while they echo Emily Dickinson's sentiment that art is a house that "tries to be haunted."

Jay Hopler's verb in "Green Squall" rings onomatopoetically, in a tropic scene: "The rain tins its romantic in the water pots." The choice of *tin* feels driven more by sonics than by logic, exactly, but "tins its romantic" makes a sly sort of sense, both echoing the metallic raindrop sound and suggesting a mood or a point of view about this sopping event.

Sometimes verbs gain descriptive force when other parts of speech are newly cast in active roles. Tracy K.

Smith evokes an ocean scene, in "Minister of *Saudade*," thusly:

> What kind of game is the sea?
>
> Lap and drag. Crag and gleam.

Lap, drag, crag, gleam—are we reading nouns or verbs, or both? This syntactical surprise, as well as two lines of monosyllables, creates something like the equivalent of "chop," making this a rough, playful ocean.

Here is Alex Lemon on the aftermath of surgery:

> Anesthesia dumb, scalpel-paste
> Rawing my tongue, I found
> Myself starfished in sky
> Spinning days.

Rawing and *starfished* are splendidly inventive, and their energetic character makes the speaker here seem raked, transformed by an extreme physical experience. The syntactical ambiguity disorients further: Is the speaker "starfished" (that is, spread-eagled) in days that spin the sky around, so he can't tell what time it is, or what day? Or does he feel like he's in the sky, spinning the days himself with a body that points in all directions? The richness of verbs and the syntactical élan with which they're used allow for a useful ambiguity.

This is the first section of Shelley's "Ode to the WEST WIND":

I

O wild West Wind, thou breath of Autumn's being,
Thou, from whose unseen presence the leaves dead
Are driven, like ghosts from an enchanter fleeing,

Yellow, and black, and pale, and hectic red,
Pestilence-stricken multitudes: O thou,
Who chariotest to their dark wintry bed

The wingèd seeds, where they lie cold and low,
Each like a corpse within its grave, until
Thine azure sister of the Spring shall blow

Her clarion o'er the dreaming earth, and fill
(Driving sweet buds like flocks to feed in air)
With living hues and odours plain and hill:

Wild Spirit, which art moving everywhere;
Destroyer and preserver; hear, oh, hear!

That is the opening movement of one of the great lyrics in the language, an astonishing poem centering around the desire to die into the world, to give oneself over entirely, to surrender into the life of things so that one might be, as the earth is, renewed—and thus, even to become that winnowing wind oneself, to *be* the vital force of things. The poem merits an alphabet of its own, but looking through the lens of the describer's art, I'll say just a few things about it here.

1. Shelley gains great power by constructing his poem as an invocation. Directly addressing the West Wind creates a sense of immediacy and of connection, some bond already extant between the speaker and what could easily be seen as an impersonal, random, and indifferent force. But by beginning "O wild West Wind, thou . . .", he's placed himself in what already seems an intimate relation. And since the word that comes next is *breath,* we're invited to think of the wind as an exhalation just as this poem is, just as our own lungs are doing in saying these initial words. Both Shelley and the reader are also "winds."

2. It's telling to look at the first and last words of line two. *Thou* is back in line two, right at the beginning. Not *you,* with its greater distance, but *Thou* with its suggestion of divinity or beloved, and the repetition of the word from the first line creates a sense of fervent prayer. The end of the line—"leaves dead"—inverts the expected order,

so that that final word falls like a lifeless hand to
the table.

3. Autumn leaves, the occasion for many a term of
praise elsewhere, become here engagingly creepy;
they're "like ghosts," and that list of colors in line
four is surely one of the more unpleasant ones
around. Yellow, black, and "hectic red" form a kind
of uncomfortable alliance, inharmonious, something that might set the teeth on edge; replace
that adjective with some other two-syllable term
for red—*glowing, burning, restless*—and almost
anything seems more attractive than *hectic.* The
fourth element in the list energizes it by depart-
ing from the color words to give us *pale*—a term
associated, of course, with illness.

4. *Dead* and *pale* have prepared the way for the
chain of terms associated with disease and decay
to follow: to see the leaves as "pestilence-stricken
multitudes" and the winged seed cold "like a
corpse within its grave" is to reveal the speaker's
state of mind, the death-steeped perception that
reads the wind as a "destroyer."

5. *Chariotest,* a fine verb, is satisfyingly thick on the
tongue. It evokes the ancient world, as if the West
Wind were a god we'd see driving splendid horses
on a Parthenon frieze. It suggests battle, the cruel
conqueror scattering the stricken multitudes
ahead of him.

6. The last line of the third stanza gives us the first indication of hope, when that "azure sister" is promised. The line leads directly into the fourth stanza, which is entirely a room full of spring, of rebirth, the earth not dead but dreaming, so that the poem now contains both forces, the destructive balanced with the promise if not the immediate prospect of beginning.

7. With these two elements introduced, the extraordinary final stanza can hold them both in balance, evoking in its outcry a world of fused duality:

> Wild Spirit, which art moving everywhere;
> Destroyer and preserver; hear, oh, hear!

And though we know this speech is addressed to the wind, those capital letters and the choice of the word *spirit* can't help but make Shelley's poem a prayer, not to any Judeo-Christian deity but to a divine animator more like Shiva, who both destroys and sustains. But it's a signature of this tempestuous Romantic temperament that he wants not to submit to God, but finally to be that divinity: "Be thou, Spirit fierce," he cries out later in the poem, "My spirit! Be thou me, impetuous one!" He wants to be the wind of words blowing into the world.

X-RAY: What lies beneath the visible? Is it possible to look beneath the green of the maple leaf to the blazing carmine sugars below, or beneath the slippery signature of the passing snake to the *s* curve of the elegant little bones? Beneath the bones? The poem, of course, has that freedom to move, as in that moment in "The Fish" when the speaker's eyes seem to probe beneath the scaled surface to entrails and swim-bladder, or in that stanza from Robert Hass's "That Music" when the consciousness of the poem seems to dive down beneath the soil to be present with the snowmelt "percolating through the roots of mountain grasses." Is Shelley looking down, beneath the gorgeous flesh of autumn—which in his ode is rotting, pestilent—to some dynamic principle at work in things, a kind of logarithm of decay and rekindling?

YIELD Everything, Force Nothing

Years circling the same circle:
the call to be first,
and the underlying want:

and this morning, look! I've finished now,
with this terrific red thing,
with green and yellow rings on it, and stars.

The contest is over:
I turned away,
and I am beautiful: Job's last daughters,
Cinnamon, Eyeshadow, Dove.

The contest is over:
I let my hands fall,
and here is your garden:
Cinammon, Eyeshadow, Dove.

—*Jean Valentine*

Jean Valentine's poems are committed to the description of interiority; their allegiance is inward, as if the poet were taking dictation from an inner voice, or transcribing a process of meditation. But they also possess a hard-won clarity, something that opens itself to us through careful attention; the poem seems to ask the reader to slow to the pace of its speaker, to move into the same kind of quiet, watchful consciousness in which one witnesses the procession of inner events.

The first stanza of of "Yield Everything" remembers a state of ambition any artist might recognize: the drive to success, and the sense of lack that underlies that drive, the longing for validation that seems insatiable. Therefore there is something funny and delightful about the line that follows it—"and this morning, look! I've finished now"—as if one *could* come to that sort of fulfillment, and the artist could say, yes, that's what I wanted to do, and stand back and dust off her hands. The made thing here sounds delightfully like a school project, and in truth the speaker thinks it's just "terrific." And thus years of being caught in a circle of ambition and unfulfilled desire are dismissed in a stanza, and brought to a close. This is such a delight, this feeling, that the speaker must tell us twice, "The contest is over."

How much time do most of us spend behaving as if we're trying to win a contest? To win money or acclaim, to have a satisfying amount of love or sex or beauty or pleasure or accomplishment—well, as Marie Howe puts it in "What the Living Do," "We want more and more and then more of it." Whatever it is.

The action of "forcing" the title points to falls away

in Valentine's last two stanzas, and what is the result? Beauty and mystery, no struggle, not trying to do anything. I cease my striving and suddenly there's a "you"—"*your* garden" now contains these mysterious daughters, with their splendid names bringing to the poem attributes of fragrance, flavor, shading, the song and movement of the dove. Job, of course, struggled and suffered, but now his daughters occupy the second half of the poem, named once (in italics, as proper names) and again, in roman type, as three nouns of pleasure and delight.

Unlike almost every other poem I've referenced here, Valentine's lovely parable is not much interested in the textures and particulars of the outside world; its specificities are here to form the sensous grounding of the inner life. But this act of representation is an act of description nonetheless, and a deeply faithful one.

A to Z, I reach the end of my lexicon and feel that my effort to describe description is happily partial, partisan, a work of advocacy. Startling, to go description-hunting and realize that I can thumb through whole books of recent poems with very little evocation of sense perception within them. Why is this the case? I declare myself here on the side of allegiance to the sensible, things as they are, the given, the incompletely knowable, never to get done or get it right or render it whole: ours to say and say. The mightiest of our resources brought to the task, to make the world real.

Permission Acknowledgments

MARK DOTY is the author of *Fire to Fire: New and Selected Poems,* which won the 2008 National Book Award. His other collections of poetry include *School of the Arts, Atlantis,* and *My Alexandria,* which won the National Book Critics Circle Award. He has also published four works of nonfiction prose, including *Dog Years* and *Heaven's Coast,* which received the PEN/Martha Albrand Award for First Nonfiction. Doty lives in New York City and on the east end of Long Island, and he teaches at Rutgers University in New Brunswick, New Jersey.

The text of *The Art of Description: World into Word* is set in Warnock Pro, a typeface designed by Robert Slimbach for Adobe Systems in 2000. Book design by Wendy Holdman. Composition by BookMobile Design and Publishing Services, Minneapolis, Minnesota. Manufactured by Versa Press on acid-free paper.